FAITH, WILL, AND GRAMMAR

PUBLICATIONS OF LUTHER-AGRICOLA-SOCIETY B 15

FAITH, WILL, AND GRAMMAR

Some Themes of Intensional Logic and Semantics in Medieval and Reformation Thought

Edited by
HEIKKI KIRJAVAINEN

HELSINKI 1986

ISBN 951-9047-20-4
ISSN 0357-3095

Vammalan Kirjapaino Oy 1986

PREFACE

These three essays have no special connection to one another. The origin of each of them is rather independent, too. However, they have a common ground in that they all elucidate certain *intensional* terms, namely those of 'knowing', 'believing', 'willing' and 'having a religious faith'.

What do we mean by an intensional term? Very briefly, semantically speaking, it means that we cannot understand the meaning of such a term by referring to the external world only. This, in turn, implies that there is a large number of conceptual elements to be taken into account in the analysis of such terms. We might call, therefore, such an analysis intensional logic. All the three essays in the present book are items of intensional logic in this wide sense. In these essays historical approaches are taken on the notions mentioned above.

Docent, Dr. Heikki Kirjavainen is a Senior Fellow in the Finnish Academy, Risto Saarinen, Licentiate in Theology, is a Junior Research scholar at the University of Helsinki and Docent, Dr. Reijo Työrinoja is an Assistant Professor at the University of Helsinki.

The writers of this study would like express their deep gratitude to Professor Simo Knuuttila who has kindly read most of the papers and has offered extremely valuable comments. To him this book is dedicated.

Our thanks also go to Mark Shackleton, Lecturer in English at the University of Helsinki, for checking the English of the text.

The Editor

CONTENTS

HEIKKI KIRJAVAINEN

THE SIMULTANEITY OF FAITH AND KNOWLEDGE: TENDENCIES IN EPISTEMIC LOGIC FROM ANTIQUITY TO HIGH SCHOLASTICISM

CONTENTS

12

1. INTRODUCTION

One of the most central themes in western epistemology has been the question concerning the relationship between religious belief and rational knowledge. If we want to clarify any of the historical solutions given to this question we will soon face this problem: how do we get at the best possible explications of those historical views? In the following I shall make some remarks concerning this methodological demand.

1.1 Formal notation

We shall use the following symbols in formulating formulae:

Intensional operators:

'K' = 'knows'
'B' = 'believes'
'J' = 'has been justified'
'T' = 'thinks'
'V' = 'is certain'
'A' = 'assents'
'M' = 'is possible'
'N' = 'is necessary'
'D' = 'doubts'
'O' = 'opines'
'W' = 'wills'

Variables

'p', 'q',... propositional variables,
'a', 'b',... individual symbols/subscripts,
'ϕ'... arbitrary formula in metalanguage,
'μ', 'μ^*'... model sets.

Logical constants

'&', 'v', '~', '⊃', '≡',
→'...intensional entailment,
'⊂'...set inclusion,
'⊢'...logical deducibility,
'ε'...membership relation.

1.2 Epistemic logic

By epistemic logic we mean the systematic logical and semantical analysis and theories concerning the expressions 'to know', 'to believe', 'to be certain', 'to opine' and the like.[1] Recently, three main problems have been discussed in epistemic logic: (1) the problem of the definition of knowledge, (2) the problem of the rationality (»logicity») of knowledge and belief and (3) the problem of the so-called KK-thesis which concerns the transitivity property of knowledge and belief. I do not want go into the details of these three problems here. I only want to point out, very briefly, that the discussion of the first problem has shown up the impossibility of defining knowledge *via* justification. This means that although the principle

$$(\text{Impl}_K) \quad K(p \supset q) \supset (Kp \supset Kq)$$

is valid in epistemic logic, the principle

$$(\text{Impl}_J) \quad K(p \supset q) \supset (Jp \supset Jq)$$

is not.

The second problem has been discussed by asking how much *rationality* we must presuppose in order to speak about »the logic» of epistemic and doxastic notions. This means that the standards of knowing and believing do not bear on arbitrary and miscellaneous sets of purely factual beliefs of people but on sets which can be handled by some rules of inference. In this sense there are conceptual rules which must be con-

---

[1] We may follow Hintikka's ideas and say that by epistemic logic we mean those logical truths which hold for expressions containing *essentially* the terms 'to know' and 'to believe' and their cognates. See Jaakko Hintikka, *Knowledge and Belief*. An Introduction to the Logic of the Two Notions. Ithaca, New York 1962; of modern discussions see W. Lenzen, *Recent Work in Epistemic Logic. Acta Philosophica Fennica*. Vol. 30, No. 1, Amsterdam 1978, p. 18—34.

sidered to be analytically true, in somewhat idealised and implicit form, for the concepts of knowledge and belief. The main such standard is the requirement of deductive closure or the principle of logical »omniscience», which can be formulated as follows

$$(DC) \quad \frac{p \supset q}{Kp \supset Kq}.$$

A corresponding principle can be stated for believing, too. It guarantees the logical coherence of our believings vs. knowledge.

The third problem concerns the transitivity of knowledge and belief. It has been argued that if a knows that p, then he »virtually» also knows that he knows that p. This means that there are no possibilities which, if actualised, would be in contradiction with anything one knows i.e. if a knows that p, then it has to be the case that in all those possible worlds which are compatible with everything a knows, a also knows that he knows that p. Using a model theoretic formulation we get

(KK)   If »$K_a p$» $\in \mu$ and if μ^* is an epistemic alternative to μ (with respect to a) in some model system, then »$K_a p$» $\in \mu^*$.

Another way of expressing the KK-thesis would be

(KK') $K_a p \supset K_a K_a p$.

In epistemic logic we naturally have some less problematic further conditions e.g. that of the possibility of knowing or believing: if p is possible for all that a knows/believes, then p is true at least in one possible world compatible with everything a knows/believes.[2]

What is interesting from the point of view of the relationship between faith and knowledge is the question whether religious beliefs are considered to be members only in doxastic alternatives, or in epistemic ones, too. This is to ask whether what is considered to be possible in religion is considered to be possibly known. It can be argued that although all

---

[2] See Hintikka (1962) p. 40—59; Lenzen (1978) p. 53, 64, 77; H. Kirjavainen, *Certainty, Assent and Belief.* An Introduction to the Logical and Semantical Analysis of Some Epistemic and Doxastic Notions Especially in the Light of Jaakko Hintikka's Epistemic Logic and Cardinal John Henry Newman's Discussion on Certitude. Publications of the Luther-Agricola-Society B 11, Helsinki 1978, p. 32—47.

one's believings are in epistemic alternatives, because a person is bound to know *that* he believes, one's beliefs are not, because *what* one believes might be incompatible with what one knows. This leads to an important problem of the simultaneity of knowledge and faith. 'Simultaneity', namely, can be understood as the soul's capability of keeping in touch with the objects of knowledge and faith. This capability is sometimes conceived as purely logical *compatibility,* sometimes as requiring specific *acts* from the part of the soul.

1.3 The constructions of epistemic and doxastic terms

There are several different syntactic constructions in connection with epistemic notions.[3] We use e.g. the expressions 'a knows that...', 'a believes that...' 'a is certain that...' etc. to carry our epistemic claim. These constructions can be understood as expressing *propositional attitudes* i.e. the relation between a subject and a proposition. Some other constructions are non-propositional e.g. 'a knows how', which is easily conceived as expressing *a skill* or *a faculty* or 'a knows who' meaning e.g. 'I know *him*' which as a direct object construction expresses *acquaintance.* Interesting cases are those that can be reduced to propositional cases e.g. 'knowing what, where, when' and perhaps also 'knowing who'.

The constructions of believing are mostly similar to those of knowing. There are, however, two interesting differences between knowledge and belief. Firstly, 'to believe in' is a construction which is not quite analogical to 'to know somebody' because it is clearly non-propositional, expressing trust or faith, which is not reducible to believing any fixed set of propositions. Another difference is that we do not use the direct object construction 'I believe him' as expressing an analogical doxastic attitude as is knowledge by acquaintance, but as expressing something cryptopropositional.

Certainty is a concept which denotes a *mental state* or *act* as well as

---

[3] Here I mainly follow the suggestions made by Hintikka in »Different Constructions in Terms of the Basic Epistemological Verbs», *The Intentions of Intentionality and Other New Models for Modalities.* Synthese Library 90, Dordrecht-Holland/Boston-U.S.A. 1975, p. 1—25; Kirjavainen (1978) p. 26—27, 97, 143.

a cognitive propositional attitude. Accordingly, if somebody says that he is certain how to drive a car it does not follow that he can drive a car.

Assent can be taken essentially as a *propositional act*. We do not assent to things but we do always assent to propositions.

Some of the conceptual differences between knowledge and belief (and also between other epistemic and doxastic notions) are reflected in questions asked in connection to these concepts. We do not say 'Why do you know?' but 'How do you know?', and correspondingly we do not say 'How do you believe?' but 'Why do you believe?'. This reveals that in the case of believing (or perhaps also of being certain) we are facing more a non-cognitive or decisional or motivational attitude than in the case of knowing where the cognitive grounds or evidence are required and where an informational attitude is at stake.

What methodological moral can be derived from these remarks? At least this: If we want to study historically epistemic and doxastic conceptions we have to observe carefully what questions are supposed to be answered in connection with those conceptions. Sometimes we see the underlying questions on behalf of the constructions used; mostly we cannot see them directly but with the help of some roundabout way and scrutiny.

1.4 Method and task

The remarks above are apt to lead to a certain general methodological view concerning the research of philosophico-historically central discussions of epistemic notions. The research has to be able to explain *why* certain conceptions have been sustained; it is not enough to give information about *what* those conceptions have been. To give an answer *why* is to give a conceptual map or model which is powerful enough to be used in explicating the variations among the logical traits of the conceptions in question. I propose the view that epistemic logic is a model of the type that enables us to specify conceptually the content or meaning of the historical solutions given in epistemic analyses.

Our task is to clarify the notion of religious faith. This implies that we ask: has faith been analysed as satisfying purely cognitive or rational conditions, or do any of its analyses point to something else? Therefore, if we want to study the relationship between faith and knowledge, we have to ask, first, whether faith, also in historical contexts, has been considered to satisfy the analytical standards of the »logic» of knowledge and belief i.e. *metalogical criteria*. By studying these criteria we can ask, secondly, whether faith has been seen as compatible or simultaneous with knowledge, or perhaps autonoumous or *sui generis*.

Therefore, we shall be looking for the historical roots of these conditions, that is, we shall be following the paths in changes of the metalogical criteria i.e. in the conditions of *truth, justification and certainty* of knowledge, belief, opinion and faith. The main question will be: *is simultaneous faith and knowledge possible according to our western philosophical tradition?* I shall restrict my task to the period from Greek Antiquity to the time of St. Thomas Aquinas.

2. PLATO AND ARISTOTLE ON BELIEF AND KNOWLEDGE

One of the most interesting explanatory views concerning the philosophy of Plato and Aristotle has emerged from the discussion which has its origin in Arthur Lovejoy's influential book *The Great Chain of Being,* where the author represented the so-called »Principle of Plenitude» as the basic explanatory factor in the western history of ideas. What the discussion on this principle has brought into focus is the importance of the role of the »statistical» modal theory and the background presuppositions of implicit teleology.[1] I shall rely on both of these explanatory factors in the following.

2.1 A Difficulty implied by the so-called Classical Definition of Knowledge

Plato's philosophy represents one of the first attempts to define systematically the notion of knowledge. In his dialogue *Theaitetos* (210c) Plato formulates this definition by saying that knowledge is true belief added to reasoning or justification *(lógos)*. With the help of this classical definition Plato tries to make a distinction between genuine knowledge *(epistéme)* and mere belief or opinion *(doxa)*. By using the familiar symbolic notation we could render this definition as follows:

$$(Df.K) \qquad K_a p = p \ \& \ J_a p \ \& \ B_a p.[2]$$

[1] See A. O. Lovejoy, *The Great Chain of Being.* A Study of the History of an Idea. Cambridge, Mass. 1948; J. Hintikka, *Time and Necessity.* Studies in Aristotle's Theory of Modality, Oxford 1973; J. Hintikka, *Knowledge and the Known.* Historical Perspectives in Epistemology, Synthese Historical Library 11, Dordrecht-Holland/Boston-U.S.A., 1974; S. Knuuttila, »Time and Modality in Scholasticism» in *Reforging the Great Chain of Being.* Studies of the History of Modal Theories. Ed. S. Knuuttila, Synthese Historical Library 20, Dordrecht-Holland/Boston-U.S.A./London-England 1981, p. 163—257; S. Knuuttila, »Modal Logic», *LMP* 1982, p. 342—357.

[2] See Lenzen (1978) p. 18—34; Plato, *Theaitetos,* 210c.

From (Df.K) three theorems immediately seem to follow:

(1) $K_a p \supset p$,

(2) $K_a p \supset J_a p$,

(3) $K_a p \supset B_a p$.

Because Plato quite clearly rejected (3) there must be in his thinking some important traits which were apt to force him to do so. Therefore, we have to look for Plato's background presuppositions in order to understand his apparent inconsistency.

Why did Plato try to maintain that the definition of knowledge entails belief but, at the same time, excludes belief? Elsewhere I have tried to argue that the answer consists of seeing that Plato was not always able to distinguish between the *class-inclusion* and the *membership of a form*.[3] My argument is, briefly, as follows: On the one hand, belief is co-existent with knowledge taken *extensionally* so that in every actual case of knowing, believing is also involved, but, on the other hand, taken *intensionally* we cannot say that the notion of belief is a part of the notion of knowledge, because these notions belong to quite different forms. This is to say that Plato should have endorsed the interpretation

(Int) $K \rightarrow B$

meaning that is in keeping with the classical definition that the notion of belief is included in the notion of knowledge. On the other hand, he did not do that but instead accepted the interpretation

(Ext) $E(K) \subset E(B)$

which states that a certain totality is divided in such a way that the cases of knowing are a sub-class of the cases of belief.[4]

---

[3] See H. Kirjavainen, *Uskon ja tiedon samanaikaisuus. Totuus-, perustelu- ja varmuusehdon esiintymisiä uskonnollisen uskon määrittelyssä antiikista korkeaskolastikkaan.* (The Simultaneity of Faith and Knowledge. The Conditions of Truth, Justification, and Certainty in the Definitions of Religious Belief from Antiquity to High Scholasticism. Publications of the Finnish Society of Theological Literature 137, Helsinki 1983, p. 32—36.

[4] Plato says that belief is »a part» of knowledge. But this 'to be a part' becomes ambiguous meaning on the one hand *intensional entailment* (or conceptual entailment) and on the other hand *extensional class-inclusion*. See also Julius Moravcsik, »Plato's Method of Division» in *Patterns in Plato's Thought,* ed. J. Moravcsik, Dordrecht-Holland/Boston-U.S.A. 1973, p. 168—191.

2.2 Different objects of epistemic faculties

But why did Plato take so fast a hold on the view that knowledge and belief are quite different forms? I think that Hintikka is right when he emphasizes the role of what he calls the implicit teleology of Plato's thought. This trait comes to light e.g. when Plato thinks that it is sufficient to separate belief from knowledge when we see that they have different *objects*. The idea is that they are two different forms (or *genera) because* they have two different objects.[5] This implies that belief and knowledge are two different faculties *(dýnameis)* of the soul, faculties which can be almost identified with the functions *(érga)* of those faculties.[6] The tacit assumption of implicit teleology works in Aristotle, too. He says e.g. that knowing the essence of health coincides with the ability of bringing about health i.e. with the art of healing. But Aristotle criticizes Plato's thought that virtue is knowledge because according to him it does not follow automatically from knowing what justice is that one brings about justice.[7]

There are some additional and important traits in Plato's concept of knowledge. According to him knowledge is a kind of *perception of the soul or intellect.* This seems to imply that when the trait of knowledge in the likeness of a faculty refers to a linguistic construction 'knowing how', the trait of knowledge in the likeness of perception refers to the construction 'knowing who' or 'knowing what' i.e. it is knowledge in the sense of *acquaintance.*[8] These acquaintances are, according to Plato

---

[5] Cf. *Republic* V, 475—480; *Timaeus* 51d; J. Hintikka, »Knowledge and its Objects in Plato» in *Knowledge and the Known. Historical Perspectives in Epistemology.* Synthese Historical Library 11, Dordrecht-Holland/Boston-U.S.A., p. 1—30; G. Santas, »Hintikka on Knowledge and Its Objects in Plato», *Patterns in Plato's Thought,* ed. J. Moravcsik (1973).

[6] »The implicit teleology of the Greeks led them to conceive of this relation with the help of concepts, images, and locutions drawn from the realm of goal-directed activities . . . knowledge and thinking are thought of as trying to 'hit' or 'reach' their objects, 'realize themselves' in these objects. . . The apparently surprising tacit *near-identification* of the objects of knowledge and belief with the *erga* of the 'faculties' of knowledge and belief is just a further consequence of the same assumptions.» (My italics) Hintikka (1974) p. 12—13.

[7] See *Metaf.* XII, 3, 1070a28—30; *Nicomachean Ethics* 1098b31—1099a3, 114b25—35.

[8] Cf. M. Hare, *Plato.* Oxford 1982, p. 31—32; Hintikka (1974) p. 21—22. There are many examples in Plato's dialogues where he seems to think that although

and Aristotle, rather something universal than individual, namely *forms* or *ideas*.

2.3 Metalogical criteria

The formula (1) which follows from the classical definition of knowledge was accepted by Plato as the condition of truth for knowledge; (1) is to be taken as one of the most intuitive metalogical criteria of knowledge.

There were, however, other and deeper reasons for accepting this criterion. Because knowledge and belief are faculties and because all faculties tend to realize *(apergázetai)*[9] their objects, exercising a faculty tends to make its object actual. In the end, however, Plato vehemently rejects this condition from belief. It is typical that Plato did not reject the condition of truth for belief not so much for the reason that the object of belief may not be actually achieved, since what is believed may be false, as for the reason that the objects of belief cannot be proper truths, namely eternal truths of the ideal world. Therefore, belief can never realize the true objects of knowledge.[10]

Furthermore, if knowing is like seeing, then in seeing the object, say b, one has all that is needed for claiming that b exists. Since the intellect »sees» the immutable ideas independently from any sensible things the »seeing» is the proof of the existence of ideas. This is to claim that if one »sees» b, then b exists and parallelly

(C.T) $\quad T_a p \supset p$

which has become known as the principle of Parmenides. Plato had some

---

knowledge is acquaintance it is not a relation between the knowing subject and a being; rather it is a relation between the subject and the object with its predicates e.g. 'knowing Socrates as poor', which allows a reduction to the construction 'knowing that Socrates is poor'.

[9] See *Republic* V, 477c—d; 476d—e; *Gorgias* 154d: *Theaitetos* 152c; Hintikka (1974) p. 11.

[10] We may have, according to Plato, some kind of knowledge of sensible things, if what is uttered is the case at the moment of the utterance. But this creates a difficulty for Plato since if everything always changes in the sense world then it never can be so when it was at the moment of the utterance. Therefore, proper truths can only be of the immutable. See *Theaitetos* 152d; 183a; Hintikka (1974) p. 62, 27—28.

difficulties, however, in accepting (C.T), because it seems to make any falsity impossible.[11]

In his Dialogue *Meno* (97a—100c) Plato says that if somebody has an eyewitness knowledge or acquaintance of the road to Larissa, or if he has only a right opinion of this road, he seems to be in both cases a person to give equally good advice concerning this matter. This means that knowledge and belief seem to be equally good ways to virtue. In fact they are not, thinks Plato, because, as I have previously said, belief cannot make its objects true. Belief and knowledge are distinguished from each other by knowledge being *infallible* (97a), since knowledge is bound to immutable (98a), whereas belief is *fallible*.[12] Furthermore, in order to have knowledge we must have an answer to the question 'What is x?' in its immutable essence. So the answer can be given only by the description of the form or idea of x. But how do we get at these answers? By having an »*orthos logos*», says Plato, by which he means a peculiar kind of inference, an inference which consists of grasping the essential form or idea. So, in order *to know* the road to Larissa it is not enough that a person has a sensible picture of this road in his soul, the picture consisting of contingent and mutable facts. In addition he must have in his soul an »orthos logos» connecting these facts to the idea of that road.[13]

2.4 Explanations and problems

Plato's thought seems circular, but is it a *circulus vitiosus* or not? He seems to claim that if knowledge and belief are different faculties they must have different objects. But then he also claims that since knowledge and belief have different objects they must be different faculties. How

---

[11] Our suggestion is mainly supported by Hintikka's argument according to which the problem of meaningful truth was highly relevant to Plato in this connection. See Hintikka (1974) p. 22—28.

[12] In *Theaitetos* 186d Plato says that knowledge does not concern the objects of experience, but concerns inferences in general. This is because the essence and truth of things seem to be possible with the help of the latter but impossible with the help of the former.

[13] Historically the most important idea of Plato was that he was not so much interested in defining all natural classes as defining what Moravcsik has called »second order natural classes» as types of human faculties and actions. Here we can see one of the historical roots of so-called »second intentions» i.e. concepts defined as e.g. epistemic faculties. See Moravcsik ed. (1973) p. 179.

do we explain this?[14] The answer seems to be that having the same object is a necessary and sufficient condition for identifying the two faculties. Therefore, the object is the primary criterion for the specification of a faculty and so the circle is not a vicious one within the Platonic framework.

There are two ingredients in those frames which explain Plato's way of thinking: the presupposition of temporally indefinite sentences and the implicit teleology. The former conception implied that the truth value of a cognitive sentence was connected to the moment of its uttering. Consequently, only the *always* true sentences could be truthfully uttered *at any time* and could be the proper object of knowledge. This is the reason why the logico-mathematical and conceptually true sentences were for Plato the proper objects of knowledge. Sentences speaking of the sensible world *(»empeiria»)* can be truthfully uttered at some moment but not at some other. Therefore they are the objects of belief.[15]

In order to be able to separate from each other the case of knowing the road to Larissa in the proper sense and only to have a right opinion of it we must be able to form an immutable expression of it. This is possible according to Plato when we have in this case something as our object which makes the faculty of knowledge work; it can only be an idea. If we have this kind of idea as the object of our intellect, then by the implicit teleology, we »use» a different faculty than mere believing. Therefore, having a faculty is tantamount to having an end and having an end is tantamount to exercising the faculty that is most appropriate to it. We may conclude that the possibility of simultaneity depends on the defining characteristics of knowledge and belief, in the case of Plato, on the different objects or ends. These characteristics seem to influence the fact that in Plato there are such metalogical criteria applied to knowledge and belief that they become exclusive and cannot be applied simultaneously. But as we saw in the case of the road to Larissa, it was not easy for Plato to distinguish the case of mere correct believing and proper knowing.

---

[14] Hintikka says in (1974) p. 27: »On one hand it suggests that if knowledge and belief can be distinguished, their objects must be different. On the other hand, it virtually forces Plato to provide different objects for knowledge and belief before he can be as much as satisfied that the two 'faculties' really are different.»

[15] On the »contextual» concept of knowledge as linked with the demand of eternal truths as objects of proper knowledge see Hintikka (1974) p. 20; compare p. 75.

Therefore, there seems to be some fluctuating possibility for simultaneous belief and knowledge. We can only say that in so far as the objects are at stake there cannot be simultaneous knowledge and belief of the same object because there cannot be any such object.

There were some important consequences derived from Platonic thought that were to dominate the discussion after him. Perhaps most important was precisely the partly hidden teleological presumption. We have to ask, therefore: (1) What efficiency did the presumption of the implicit teleology have in the epistemic analyses after Plato? Our next question concerning the later discussion is: (2) Is it possible for one person to have, at the same time, knowledge and belief of the same object? To answer this question in different historical cases presupposes the clarification not only of what the thinker in question personally says, but, as I already hinted in the Introduction, what metalogical criteria he in fact uses.

2.5 The idea of scientific knowledge in Aristotle

According to Aristotle the soul possesses truth in five ways: (i) scientifically, which is to know by demonstration, (ii) intuitively *(nous),* which is to know the principles, (iii) by wisdom, (iv) by art and (v) by deliberative reason. The first two belong to the theoretical soul, the rest to the evaluative soul.[16]

Knowledge in the proper sense was for Aristotle as for Plato scientific knowledge. What does it consist of? Firstly, it concerns the immutable and essential characteristics of natural classes. Since the difference between the accidental and essential characteristics of a being is thought absolute according to Aristotle, scientific knowledge is always conceptual and not purely empirical.

Secondly, in *Anal. post.* (71b10) Aristotle says that in order to have knowledge (1) we must have the cause (*aitia*). In addition, we must (2) see that the case cannot be otherwise. To refer to the causes is to explain (or to justify). Therefore, scientific knowledge is to explain something via rational causes. But it also presupposes that its object is something which cannot be otherwise.[17] The necessity of knowledge goes along

---

[16] See *Nicomachean Ethics* VI, 3—6.

[17] In *Nicomachean Ethics* (VI, 3, 18—24) Aristotle says that when contingent

with the temporal generality: what is necessary is what is always. Therefore, we know scientifically when we have an explanation which handles
the object of our knowledge as a deductive consequence from some
intuitively certain premisses. This kind of knowledge satisfies both the
condition of causality (demonstration) and the condition of necessity (omnitemporality).

Aristotle also says that knowledge must be true.[18] By this he, of
course, means that what is known must be the case. Therefore, we can
conclude that Aristotle accepts both the condition of truth and the condition justification for knowledge. Genuine knowledge is such that it is
true and has a demonstration as its explanation. What then is the role
of the condition of belief for Aristotle?

2.6 The simultaneity of knowledge and belief

At first sight the basic difference between knowledge and belief seems
to be in the different objects they have. As Aristotle says:

> Knowledge and its object differ from opinion and its object in that knowledge
> is of the universal and proceeds by necessary propositions; and that which is
> necessary cannot be otherwise; but there are some propositions which, though
> true and real, are also capable of being otherwise. Obviously it is not knowledge
> that is concerned with these; if it were, that which is capable of being other-
> wise would be incapable of being otherwise.[19]

This view seems to imply that there cannot be any proper knowledge of
contingent sensible things; these are objects of opinion or belief only.
Then the question arises: is the standpoint of Aristotle precisely the same
as that of Plato?

Aristotle's answer is that if somebody thinks that some attribute belongs to a being, then though his thought were true, it is not knowledge

---

things are not actually seen we cannot know whether they exist or not. Therefore,
the object of knowledge has to be something necessary and eternal.

[18] Although Aristotle criticizes Plato's view that virtue is knowledge he himself
is also tied to implicit teleology. Aristotle says that only what is actually existent can
be the object of knowledge. If the existent object vanishes *the knowledge also vanishes*.
See *Nicomachean Ethics* 1098b 31—1099a 3; 1146b 25—35; *Metaphysics* XII, 3, 1070a
28—30 *Categories* 7, 7b 27; Hintikka (1974) p. 11, 41, 48; Knuuttila (1981) p. 166,
footnote 7.

[19] See *Anal. post.* I, 33, 88b 30—35.

unless the attribute in question belongs to that being *essentially*. There
are two possibilities for us to see the essential attribution: by intuition
and by demonstration. If we cannot have an essential attribution, then
we might have true or false belief, but not knowledge.[20] Therefore, Aristotle's view deviates from that of Plato in that the criterion of the difference between knowledge and belief is not so much in different objects
but in different ways by which those objects are achieved.

It follows that we may have the same object for belief and knowledge,
but not at the same time and for the same person. For different persons
the same thing can be at the same time, an object of belief for the one,
and an object of knowledge for the other.[21] If the persons do not *see*
the same object in the same way, they do not exercise the same faculty.
Therefore, we understand that in Aristotle the object as the defining factor
of faculty has somewhat weakened. End and faculty begin to be conceptually more independent than in Plato.

2.7 Certainty and assent

If somebody does not have an explanation, then he only believes. But
if he then thinks that his belief is certain, he in fact gives up to take it
as a mere belief. As Aristotle says:

> ...for opinion ...is uncertain. Besides, no one thinks that he is »opining»
> when he thinks that a thing cannot be otherwise; he thinks that he has
> knowledge.[22]

Thus, Aristotle seems to recognize a different epistemic attitude for
first person utterances: if a person says as it to himself 'I believe that
p and it cannot be that non-p' he has a very strong belief. This first person belief converts to knowledge because it is certain. It is interesting

---

[20] See *Anal. post.* I, 33, 89a 18—25: »The solution is probably this. If you
apprehend propositions which cannot be otherwise in the same way as you apprehend
the definitions through which demonstrations are effected, you will have not opinion
but knowledge; but if you only apprehend that the attributes are true and not that
they apply in virtue of the essence and specific nature of their subject, you will have
not true knowledge but an opinion...»

[21] See *Anal. post.* I, 33, 89a 34—38; *ibid.* 89b 5; Sir David Ross, *Aristotle.* University Paperback 65, 1968, p. 49.

[22] See *Anal. post.* I, 33, 89a 7—8. Cf. *Nicomachean Ethics* 1146b 26: »Then
some believers do not doubt but think that they distinctly know.»

that these kinds of beliefs are on a par with axioms and principles of intuitive *nous*. Although these strong beliefs do not satisfy the condition of justification they tend to satisfy the condition of truth. Also belonging to their conceptual structure is the fact that they are a kind of meta-beliefs or iterated beliefs since they imply a sort of evaluation of the certainty or truthfulness of a belief.

Aristotle does not speak about belief in the context of theoretical reason only. There is also an act which in the context of practical reason corresponds to believing. This act comes very close to *prohairesis* but is also somewhat different. Aristotle expresses this by saying that our deliberating faculty *(dianoia)* assents *(sygkatathésetai)* to the principle that of two alternatives what is more excellent is also more desirable.[23] This is to say that assent is a conceptual rule by which we may say that what is better is also more desirable and what is more probable is also *verisimilior*. By steps the role of assent comes to be the basic mental act by which we evaluate how strong or plausible our doxastic attitudes are and by which we choose our way of action.[24]

Because knowledge properly understood is knowledge of essences, the appropriate construction for knowledge is that of acquaintance. This view is shared by both Plato and Aristotle. But Aristotle emphasizes that the species of scientific knowledge is not to be distinguished by the specific object only, though the faculty of knowing depends on the capability of achieving a certain end. 'Knowing what' (acquaintance), 'knowing how' (faculty) and scientific knowledge (demonstration) are all linked together by implicit teleology, but with an effort of more distinctive analysis than in Plato. This is the answer to the question (1) in 2.4.

We have also seen that Aristotle did accept the condition of truth and justification, but he did not accept the condition of belief of the classical definition of knowledge, except in a qualified sense of first person strong belief. Besides, contraries are (ordinary) belief and demonstration, rather than knowledge and belief as such. This is the answer to the question (2) in 2.4.

---

[23] See *Topics* III, 1, 116a 3, 11—12; cf. H. Wolfson, *The Philosophy of the Church Fathers*. Faith, Trinity, Incarnation. Cambridge, Mass. and London, England 1976, p. 116.

[24] The Stoics seemed to think that there are such iterated beliefs like 'believe to believe'. They also seemed to think these act as assents. See Wolfson (1976) p. 116, footnote 22.

3. THE ORIGIN OF THE AUGUSTINIAN TRADITION

When we move on from antiquity to the era of so-called Christian Philosophy we see that it becomes very important to find a fitting role for the notion of faith on the map of epistemic concepts. In this seeking the classic problem of knowledge and faith was paradigmatically formulated by St. Augustine. He was forced to face the problem in the following form: If believing *(doxa)* belongs to the lower level than knowledge *(epistéme)* because it does not consist of seeing something immutable and eternal, but of hearing something temporal and contingent, how can we relate religious believing (faith) to genuine knowledge?

3.1 The Definition of Believing and the Problem of Faith

St. Augustine seems to keep initially the platonistic conception according to which genuine knowledge is the knowledge of an eyewitness as compared to believing which is based on hearsay only and is, as St. Augustine says, »blind», i.e. knowledge only in the secondary sense.[1] On the other hand he says that in spite of its hearsay character, believing is connected with thinking. So we get as a definition:

> (*Df.B*cred)   Believing is nothing else than thinking with an assent.[2]

The question, then, is whether there are any peculiarities for the notion of religious faith.

---

[1] Cf. *Epistolas* 147, 2.7—3.8 (*PL* 33, 599—600); *De civitate Dei* XI, 3. See also R. A. Markus, »Reason and Illumination», *The Cambridge History of Later Greek and Early Medieval Philosophy*. (LGEMP) Ed. A. H. Armstrong, Cambridge 1969, p. 349.

[2] »Credere nihil aliud est quam cum assensione cogitare», *De praedest. sanctorum* 2, 5 (*PL* 44, 963).

Firstly, it is important to note that according to St. Augustine faith has an essential link with the will. As he says:

> Does anybody believe, if he does not will — or is he unbelieving, although he wills? That kind of an attitude is absurd: believing is to admit that the word is true and admitting is an activity of the will.[3]

This suggestion belongs to the discussion concerning the locutions 'believe in God' of 'have faith in God'. St. Augustine's main idea concerning the notion of religious faith seems to be that it presupposes and act of will seemingly independent of rational reasons: without an act of will it would not be religious faith, but perhaps opinion or ordinary belief. It has been said sometimes that this idea is purely biblical and does not have any roots in Greek Antiquity, having its roots rather in the biblical use of language (e.g. *'pistis'*). This, I think, is a wrong explanation. We will return to this question in 3.4, but it should already be stated here that if one does not connect the will with scientific rational reasons, then there is much evidence for connecting it at least implicitly (or conceptually) with the rational end of man.

The objects of religious faith, in contrast to mere believing or opining, are according to St. Augustine non-perceptional truths; in this sense they are like divine forms or ideas.[4] This conception, however, needs some qualifications before St. Augustine can adopt it to the body of his thought. He makes, therefore, some important classifications. The objects of understanding, on the whole, consist of the following classes: (i) *historical facts* which can be believed, but never properly understood *(intellecta),* (ii) *mathematical and logical truths* which can be both believed and understood; this means that in this case believing is *ipso facto* understanding, (iii) *theological truths* in which case we have to believe them first in order to understand them later. It is easy to see, now, that St. Augustine's most difficult epistemological problem in connection to

---

[3] See *De spiritu et littera* 31, 54. St. Augustine discusses in this context of the locution 'believe in word' which is tantamount to assenting to revelation of the form 'believe in God'.

[4] The existence of ideas is used to refute epistemological scepticism: the intellect immediately grasps some truths which are immutable, necessary, universal and absolutely certain. This means that the illumination is not only the source of the concepts but the criterion of truth, too. See *De Trinitate* IV, 15, 20 (*PL* 42, 901—902); *De civitate Dei* XI, 3.

faith was to reconciliate between classes (i) and (iii).[5] How did he do it, because first he seems to support quite the opposite?

If there are truths which can be believed but not understood, then there could be counter-examples for the formula

(4) $B_a p \supset K_a p,$

i.e. counter-examples satisfying the formula

(5) $B_a p \,\&\, \sim K_a p.$

But on the other hand St. Augustine seems to accept the Platonic formula

(3) $K_a p \supset B_a p,$

because class (iii) is such that believing is a presupposition for understanding i.e.

(6) $\sim B_a p \supset \sim K_a p.$

In order to avoid an inconsistency between (5) and (6) St. Augustine is, therefore, forced to make a sharp distinction between classes (i) and (iii); they cannot concern the same kind of objects. Accordingly, it seems to follow that the notions of religious faith and believing in general can be kept separated from each other merely by pointing to a different kind of objects. And as I said, the objects of faith resemble the objects of knowledge, the objects of believing, in turn, being contingent and temporal things. But then the problem arises: what, in the last analysis, does the formula (6) mean, because it is a formulation of the famous Augustinian thesis »*Nisi credideritis, non intelligetis*«?[6] How can we say that

---

[5] There are some terminological usages which are important to mention here: 'scire', 'cognoscere' and 'intelligere' usually signify the same. But in some contexts they differ in meaning. 'Intelligere' sometimes means *apprehension,* which is in a way a semantic illumination not, however, very distinct from an epistemic illumination. *Typically* St. Augustine says that we (1) know (scire) *the objects* of perception, (2) understand mentally (intelligere) the spiritual objects and (3) do not apprehend (apprehendere) God. See *De diversis questionibus* LXXXIII, 48 (*PL,* 40, 31). The present *scientia* is also of a lower level than the future understanding. See e.g. *De civ. Dei* XXII, 29.

[6] St. Augustine has taken this formula from Isaiah 7: 9 which in *Septuaginta* uses the term 'intelligere' for 'permanere'. Cf. *Enarrationes in Psalmos* 118, *Sermo*

understanding in some sense presupposes believing but not the other way round? What is basically the connection between faith and understanding?

3.2 Three possible prevalences

The main difficulty in the analysis of St. Augustine's philosophy of believing and knowing seems to hide in the confusion of epistemic and semantic roles of faith. Three important suggestions are to be made concerning St. Augustine's line of thought. Firstly, we could think that St. Augustine is taking faith as an explicit *means* to an end, namely, to understanding. In the same sense we usually think of various things as epistemologically necessary preparations of gaining knowledge. These preparations may be causally, but not conceptually linked with knowledge. Secondly, we could suggest that faith simply becomes transformed into vision, so that the metalogical conditions of knowing will be satisfied. But then the states of faith and knowledge could still be temporally successive. Thirdly, we could take St. Augustine's view as indicating that faith somehow illuminates what one already knows by other means.

Let us look at the first suggestion. It is not quite clear whether St. Augustine understood the relation between understanding and believing by faith as a conceptual or a causal one; typically he seems to mix both together. If so, there is an interpretation of (6) which entails that believing is causally a necessary condition for achieving understanding, and, that believing implies such conceptual ties which are necessary for a (deeper) understanding of what one already knows. Thus the first suggestion is mingled with the third one.

It is important to remember, in this connection, that our possible error in interpreting St. Augustine's thoughts would be that we would like to make much too sharp a distinction between a causal and a conceptual connection of believing and understanding. But if these two are not to be separated very distinctively then the implicit and explicit teleology of St. Augustine's thinking are also inseparable. I think that this question can be clarified by asking: in what sense, if any, did St. Augustine accept formula (4), because, if he did then he yields to a tentative equivalence of faith and understanding (knowledge); and this equivalence cannot be explained purely in causal terms.

18, 3 (*CC* 40, 1724); comp. *De Trin.* VII, 6, 12; IX, 1, 1; XV, 2, 2 (*PL* 42, 946; 961; 1057—8); *Epist.* 120, 2 (*PL* 33, 452).

3.3 Explicit teleology

It is quite obvious, however, that an explicit teleology is at work in St. Augustine's thought. Like Plato and Aristotle he thinks that human beings are directed to the supreme good. St. Augustine's standpoint differs e.g. from that of Aristotle, because when Aristotle says that man's rational will naturally turns into a praxis without alternatives in a concrete situation *(prohairesis)*, St. Augustine says that this praxis is brought about by faith which operates through love.[7]

Explicit teleology implies that faith and understanding are independent from each other. St. Augustine thinks that the following statements are compatible: '$B_{t0}p$', '$\sim K_{t0}p$', '$K_{t1}p$'. Their compatibility, in turn, presupposes that faith and knowledge are temporally successive states. But then, because faith$_{t0}$ and not-knowing$_{t0}$ are compatible, it would follow that (4) is not true as a conceptual implication. And this, of course, would indicate that St. Augustine thought of faith and knowledge as temporally successive and not simultaneous states, and consequently that understanding does not imply a purely conceptual tie to faith.

Some evidence seems to give slight confirmation both to the hypothesis of a causal and to the hypothesis of a conceptual tie in (4) at the same time. Firstly, St. Augustine says that faith *in statu viae* and seeing *in patria* are temporally successive states. But secondly, he speaks about the seed and plant as participating in the same form; he purports to say that the state of the seed is that of believing and the state of the plant is that of seeing (knowing). This means that although the object of faith and knowledge is in some sense the same, the epistemic attitudes themselves are successive states of mind; faith somehow transforms into vision. And so the second prevalent interpretation of St. Augustine would be correct. Then we could not imagine that faith is already some kind of knowledge or understanding; at least, this could be true in a rudimentary sense, but not totally.[8]

---

[7] See e.g. *In tract. Iohannis ev.* XX, 11: »fides quae per dilectionem operatur»; *De civ. Dei* XVIII, 18; XIX, 4; XXII, 29. Faith is a product of will, not of purely natural will, but of will based on God's eternal election which causes that man to become directed to God as his supreme good. By his will a man can consent to believe the divine truths as well as make a decision to will something contrary to his natural desires. Cf. *De spiritu et litt.* 31, 54; 33; *De Trin.* XI, 28 (*PL* 41, 342).

[8] Cf. *De civ. Dei* XXII, 29: »... non dico quod iam video, sed dico quod credo

3.4 Implicit teleology

Explicit teleology does not, however, exhaust St. Augustine's conception of faith. We could in fact ask: is there any sense in which faith turns into seeing, not only by producing causally the vision of God as a consequence of faith, but *by being itself such a vision*? Does the implication in (4) express, not a temporally successive and causal, but a conceptual tie between faith and understanding? The question can be studied, I think, by clarifying the metalogical criteria included in (4) by St. Augustine.

St. Augustine's main idea concerning the illumination is no doubt it is a divine guarantee for human knowledge. The illumination gives to knowledge the certainty it needs. But because the truths of the Scripture are illuminated they are certain, too. There may be some truths of faith which are in principle dubitable. As St. Augustine says:

> So long as this faith is sound and certain we cannot justly be reproached if we have doubts about some matters where neither sense nor reason give clear perception, where we have received no illumination from the canonical Scriptures and where we have not been given information by witnesses whom it would be irrational to distrust.[9]

These »matters» of faith are dubitable, because they do not satisfy the criteria of ordinary knowledge. But more important is that St. Augustine puts »clear perception», illumination from the Scripture and true witnesses in a parallel position.[10] This hints that the illumination in Scripture is the epistemic guarantee of truth. This is to say that faith satisfies at least the condition of truth transforming itself into knowledge in this way.

But this is not the whole story. If there is any implicit teleology, it has to be the case that we cannot describe faith and vision independently.

...»; *Sermo* 43, 6, 7 (*PL* 38, 257); *De Trin,* XIV, 1, 3, (*PL* 42, 1037); *De civ. Dei* XI, 2; XXII, 29; *Conf.* XIII, 29.

[9] »... qua salva atque certa de quibusdam rebus, quas neque sensu neque ratione percepimus neque nobis per scripturam canonicam claruerunt nec per testes, quibus non credere absurdum est, in nostram notitiam pervenerunt, sine iusta reprehensione dubitamus.» *De civ. Dei* XIX, 18.

[10] In *De civ. Dei* XI, 3 St. Augustine e.g. first says that there are truths which we have to know for our own good, but which are not *present* to our exterior or interior sense. However, these truths can be present to somebody and this is why we have to accept them by authority.

So, faith has to imply some kind of analytic ties or norms of meaning imposed on the attitude of knowing i.e. faith delivers a kind of conceptual integration and interpretation what we already know by natural means. This is not merely faith transforming into knowledge, firstly, because faith is composing a *condition* for knowledge, although not a causal condition, but a conceptual one:

> And yet the mind of man, the natural seat of his reason and understanding, is itself weakened by long-standing faults which darken it. It is too weak to cleave to that changeless light and to enjoy it; it is too weak even to endure that light. It must first be renewed and healed day after day so as to become capable of such felicity. And so the mind had to be trained and purified by faith;[11]

Secondly, the objects of faith and vision are to be identified as nearly, if not exactly, the *same*. Therefore there is some kind of a continuity between them:

> Therefore the power of those eyes will be extraordinary in its potency ... in the sense of having the ability to see the immaterial. And it may be that this extraordinary power of sight was given for a time even in this mortal to the eyes of the holy man Job ... no Christian doubts that it is with those eyes of the heart, or mind, that God will be seen, when he is seen.[12]

However, it appears as if the same objects which we now see dimly in faith will be seen clearly in the future vision.[13]

At first sight one is tempted to acknowledge here that the semantic and epistemic role of understanding seem to go in opposite directions: in order to believe theological truths, says St. Augustine, one has to understand the meanings of words, but, in order to understand something in any proper or deeper sense one has to have faith.[14] The point is that according to St. Augustine this something which is to be believed by faith seems to have a role of a semantic apprehension, too. It is both a kind of »sense» and »mental process» as he says:

---

[11] Cf. *De civ. Dei* XI, 2.

[12] Cf. *De civ. Dei* XXII, 29.

[13] The activity in future beatific vision surpasses all understanding; therefore, it is not easy to say what exactly is the object of the present faith and future vision. A little later St. Augustine, however, says that the present object of faith is a truth which is to be seen immaterially in the future. Cf. *De civ. Dei* XXII, 29 (*CC* 861).

[14] Cf. *Enarr. in Ps.* 118, *Sermo* 18, 3, 25—30 (*CC* 40, 1724).

> There are other matters which are perceived by the mind and the reason: and such perception is rightly described as a kind of sense; and that is why the term *sententia* denotes a mental process.[15]

So, it is not only that faith offers to the intellect the kind of objects as in (i) and in (iii) that cannot be understood scientifically i.e. by demonstration, but faith also seems to make everything else *more* understandable by linking everything to what is apprehended by faith as a set of semantical norms. This amounts to a principle like

> (B/K)   a knows that p, but a does not properly understand it, unless he believes it by faith and under the interpretation that q.

But this sounds very obscure indeed. Faith seems to be a condition for better understanding of that which is the object of understanding and also, at the same time, an enlightening factor for something else. In other words, we cannot separate from each other the case where somebody becomes more enlighted by believing something that he already somehow understands, and the case where by believing something one comes to understand something else. As I said the semantic and epistemic role of the illumination seem to overlap here.

Our conclusion, then, is that faith gives some kind of an insight which is both of a semantic and epistemic nature i.e. of the nature (B/K). Therefore, there would be at least a weak acceptance of (4); and then it follows from (4) and from (3) that between faith and understanding there holds a weak non-material equivalence relation i.e. a conceptual tie which could be formulated thus:

$$(*) \qquad B\phi \supset K\phi.$$

The formula (*) expresses what we could call faith as rudimentary understanding, or, faith as insight. This, I think, is roughly what is implied by the Augustinian implicit teleology. Faith is a form of conceptual information which has *epistemic and semantic clarity*. Together with an idea of the participation of the same form in faith and vision this speaks for the hypothesis of the conceptual tie between faith and understanding. And then (4) is not only an argumentative or material implication de-

---

[15] St. Augustine typically identifies here also Christ, *logos,* way, immaterial light, goal, renewal day by day and learning by the interior perception. See *De civ. Dei* XI, 2—3.

scribing a causal connection between faith and vision thus expressing the explicit teleology, but rather it expresses the implicit teleology. And this entails, or course, that faith not only *gives* understanding, but also *means* understanding.

3.5 Metalogical Criteria

St. Augustine's position in the epistemic discussion is thus reflected by some metalogical trends, which mean that a new kind of epistemic notion enters the scene.

Firstly, it is clear that the condition of truth for faith is accepted by St. Augustine i.e.

(1') $B^{faith}_a p \supset p$.

Secondly, the Platonic and Aristotelian *orthos logos* condition (2), which in the classical sense expresses the reason or explanation (usually in the form of syllogistic reasoning) for the known, now acquires a new meaning. Because Christ is identified with *logos* the condition (2) will describe sapiential knowledge or understanding: a person understands in the real sense only if he has the »light of faith»[16], which means intuition or insight producing semantic clarity or conceptual information. This means that the classical condition of justification of scientific knowledge as being demonstrability by syllogistic reasoning is put aside and room is made for a more semantic way of considering the justification of knowledge. It follows that if we compare the classical definition of knowledge (Df.K) with the Augustinian conception we see that '$J_a p$' is almost substituted by '$B^{faith}p$'. This view is further confirmed when we recall that according to St. Augustine most of the revealed truths are

---

[16] This »light» is called *lumen fidei, lux securitatis*. Cf. *De civ. Dei* XI, 3; VIII, 7: »Lumen autem mentium esse dixerunt ad discenda omnia eundem ipsum Deum, a quo facta sunt omnia.» XXII, 29: »Rather in that new age the faith, by which we believe, will have a greater reality for us than the appearance of material things which we see with our bodily eyes.» See also: *Contra academicos* III, 19, 42; *De libero arbitrio* II, 12, 33; II, 37; *De Trinitate* IX, 7, 12; XIII, 1; XV, 13; *De magistro* 38, 40; *De div. quaest.* LXXXIII 42, 2; compare R. A. Markus, »Reason and Illumination», *LGEMP,* p. 364; E. Serene, »Demonstrative Science», *LMP,* p. 499: H. A. Wolfson, *The Philosophy of the Church Fathers. Faith, Trinity, Incarnation,* Cambridge Massachusetts and London England 1976, p. 115.

undemonstrable.[17] Although this creates the permanent problem of whether there could be simultaneous knowledge and faith of the same thing, this also supports the inclination of using the truths of faith as satisfying the condition of justification precisely because they are based on *logos*. So, if we take 'J_ap' in the Platonic or Aristotelian sense the St. Augustine interpretation abandons it form faith. But if we take into consideration his new interpretation, then he seems to accept a formula like

(2') $B^{faith}_a p \supset J_a p$.

In this sense the classical justification condition has acquired a new interpretation based on *logos* and *authority*.

Thirdly, because faith is based on the divine illumination it acquires an important role as a metalogical criterion of the real knowledge (sapientia). This means that the classical Platonic criterion (3), which in St. Augustine is a consequence of the acceptance of (6), is strengthened by the qualification of

(3') $K_a p \supset B^{faith}_a p$.

This means that real knowledge is always connected with the efforts to achieve divine teaching in the soul. The typical Augustinian emphasis on the inseparability of virtue, philosophy and theology is a consequence thereof.

The picture of St. Augustine's epistemic thinking we get is expressed by the well known programme of *fides quaerens intellectum*.[18] Faith, being a kind of *motion,* equals an implicit teleology which makes real understanding possible. This motion, however, is not only outward explicit motion of a moral nature, but an implicit conceptual connection between faith and real knowledge so that faith becomes rudimentary knowledge. In a sense this means that faith has a fluctuating status

---

[17] »And since we cannot supply this rational proof of those matters — for they are beyond the powers of the human mind —»; ». . . (marvels) for which the human reason can supply no explanation, but which certainly exist and seem to contradict the rational order of nature». *De civ. Dei* XXI, 5.

[18] In answering the critics of Consentius St. Augustine says that we have to occupy rational clarification not in order to displace faith, but in order that »with the help of the light of reason we would understand to what we earlier firmly adhered by faith». See *Epistolas* 120, 2 (*PL* 33, 452).

between belief and knowledge: it is, at the same time, absolutely certain, but not necessary — *ex auditu* and enigmatic, but illuminated. Faith is like a wedge between belief and knowledge tending to satisfy both the metalogical criteria of belief and the metalogical criteria of knowledge. Therefore, it is clear that there can be simultaneous faith and knowledge, because faith is knowledge.

The most important trait in this new epistemic category is that it includes, in a sense, a class of *unknown contingent truths* which can be brought into the circle of reason by a firm and faithful attitude of faith, although not yet by an empirical science in the modern sense.

4. FAITH AND MYSTICAL KNOWLEDGE IN NEO-PLATONISM

In Christian Neo-Platonism faith becomes reoriented and reinterpreted by being even more separated from purely cognitive categories. Consequently, it cannot be thoroughly analysed with the criteria of epistemic logic. Two traits are important to be remembered here: Firstly, the causal and ontological are generally inseparable from the conceptual and logical: e.g. the interpretation of motion coincides very strictly with conceptual distinctions made in the scheme of emanation. It follows that faith acquires a new interpretation by being understood as a causally unifying factor.[1] Secondly, the highest reality, God, is not achieved by normal cognitive means at all; so, we cannot have any entirely adequate concepts of God either. Therefore, a new element, namely that of a mystical object, is brought into the epistemic discussion. For the notion of faith this means that faith has an object which is peculiar to it and is to be understood as a mental state of awareness of that object.[2]

---

[1] The coincidence of causality and knowing has its roots in the Platonic conception in the 6th and 7th books of the *Republic* where Plato says that to know being is to know the good according to which every thing is created (509b, 511). To this another Platonic conception was added, now ontologically interpreted, namely, that all being is to be deduced from only one principle. Therefore, according to the Neo-Platonists, causality and deducibility coincide. See Proclos, *Elementatio theologica,* 7, Ed. E. R. Dodds, Oxford 1963; Pseudo-Dionysios, *De mystica theologia,* Enchiridion asceticum coll., Rouet de Journel et Dutilleul 1947, EA 1054/9, 1045D. On this coincidence between causality and knowability (i.e. deducibility) Gersh e.g. says: »It must be admitted that these two senses (i.e. active cognition of things and respectivity to cognition) are not always clearly distinguished in the sources — indeed in some arguments they amount to precisely the same thing.» Stephen Gersh, *From Iamblichius to Eriugena.* An Investigation of the Prehistory and Evolution of the Pseudo-Dionysian Tradition, Leiden 1978, p. 267.

[2] Plotin speaks about the indefinability of God by saying that because God produces all beings He himself is none of them. He is not a being, a quality, a quantity, an intellect or a soul. He is not in motion or at rest, not in time or in any place. He

4.1 »Hénosis»

In non-Christian Neo-Platonism e.g. Proclos thought that believing is a kind of *»theurgic»* activity which leads into union with higher reality *(hénosis).*[3] This notion of belief, although of Platonic origin, is of a slightly different kind than the Platonic notion of belief as directed to the sensual world and being by nature contextual and relativistic.

The unifying role of faith in Christian Neo-Platonism is a synthesis of the themes of acquaintance and causality in the epistemic discussion in antiquity. Although faith is not cognitive vision, it has causally, as was now considered, an immediate contact with its object. This view was a natural consequence from the traditional acquaintance conception of knowledge. Because, ontologically, there is no sharp distinction between the causal and the conceptual, the condition of truth for faith will thus be accepted. In this sense faith is itself a link in the causal chain; there could not be any faith without its cause which is, in turn, the object of faith existing in reality.

Typically this way of thinking is formed in the Neo-Platonic metaphysical frames e.g. by Pseudo-Dionysios. He tried to show that there are two quite different methods of achieving God: the discursive *(katafatic)* and the mystical *(apofatic)*. But although these methods are different they do not imply any ontological exclusion of the conceptual from the causal.[4]

---

is above all forms and we cannot apply any terms to him. See *Enneades* VI, 9, 3, 39, The Loeb Classical Library, Ed. A. H. Armstrong, London 1966, Vols. V, VI; Cf. also Pseudo-Dionysios, *De divinis nominibus,* VII, 3; II, 7, 11, Enchiridion Patristicum coll., M. J. Rouet de Journel, 1947, EP 2280/5; *De myst. theol.,* III, IV, V; Gregory of Nyssa, *Contra Eunomium, II (XIIB/XIII) 89 (PG* 45, 940D—941A, 1, 252, 24—243, 17); I. P. Sheldon-Williams, »St. Gregory of Nyssa», *LGEMP,* p. 455; *ibid.,* »The Pseudo-Dionysios», *LGEMP,* 457—472; Stephen Gersh, *From Iamblichius to Eriugena.* An Investigation of the Prehistory and Evolution of the Pseudo-Dionysian Tradition, Leiden 1978, p. 17—18, 82—83, 90—91.

[3] In Neo-Platonism it was customary to equate faith with an act of intellect which transcends knowledge and contains a mystical union *(synafé).* This view is based on Plato's *State* 511E. Compare Proclos, *Theologia Platonis,* I, Ed. Saffrey-Westerink, Paris 1968, p. 110. See also W. Beierwaltes, »Der Begriff 'unum in nobis' bei Proklos», *Die Metaphysik im Mittelalter,* Miscellanea medievalia, Band 2. Berlin 1963, p. 255—266.

[4] According to Neo-Platonism the ability to transcend the knowledge of accidences and to know the substance in itself is based on *eros* and *pistis* which are,

4.2 »Epignosis»

The other essential trait in faith is that it is mystical awareness. As I have previously said there is a difference between two the methods of grasping the higher reality. God in his *ousia* is unachievable, only in his *dynameis* God can be achieved. Man's supreme goal, it is true, is to gain knowledge of God. But man's cognitive possibilities are limited to the so-called *»katafatic theology»* only i.e. what can be said of God using either those forms which are exemplified in the world as genera (speaking of God metaphorically or analogically) or using those forms which are not exemplified in the world as genera (speaking of transcendent forms: e.g. being, sameness, otherness, rest and motion).[5]

The highest point we can get by using the katafatic method is to understand the totality of forms *(pléroma)* which is identical with the totality of *logoi (paradeigmata).* The human intellect, however, cannot achieve this totality in its unity *(Logos),* because the intellect is limited *(sapientia stulta).* So, *the unity of Logos* can only be achieved by another method of theology, by the *apofatic* method. But using this method God cannot be described by any discursive way, because He necessarily contains contradictions. Accordingly, God in his essence *(ousia)* is »darkness» to the discursive thinking and the objects of faith are according to the apofatic method expressions having the status of mystical statements. In order to achieve God the human intellect has to surpass the borders of normal coherent and discursive thinking. This surpassing is »epignosis» i.e. faith. Pseudo-Dionysios describes faith by saying that

---

at the same time, the forces of the conceptual and real »motion». See e.g. Sheldon-Williams, *LGEMP,* p. 471: »... the erotic cycle which perpetually proceeds from God through the Hierarchies, the intelligible, the sensible, the animate, and the material, impressing its nature upon all, and in a symmetrical return, as 'unifying power' *(dynamis henopoios),* gathers together all hierarchically into the One.» The Neo-Platonic triad: *ousia — dynamis — energeia* corresponds to the three categories: mystical theology — katafatic theology — symbolic theology. While faith is to be located mainly in the first category, eros is part of them all. See Gersh (1978) p. 267, 270, 278.

[5] The Neo-Platonists tried to understand the intellect as the Form of forms, but when applied to God this meant that the purported Form transcended all the metaphysical categories. See Gersh (1978) p. 94—97 (footnote 61); 105—106; 267—268; Porphyrios, *Isagoge,* 7, 21—23; Jan Pinborg, *Logik und Semantik im Mittelalter.* Stuttgart Bad Canstatt 1972, p. 39—40.

it has as its object not only the divine *logoi,* but also the divine *Logos;* elsewhere he also says:

> Because knowledge is a unity between the knower and the known ... so the true believer will never be torn away from his home fireside which is the true faith, faith in which he has a lasting, unshakable, immutable certainty. Because he who knows that he is one with the Truth, knows also that he is on the right way ... he has stepped out from error with the help of true faith which is directed to the Essence.[6]

The peculiar nature of faith, then, is to be aware of the darkness of God, although it is not possible to describe this object in any way. This means that it is not possible to reduce the knowing which comes through faith to acquaintance: 'knowing that' is not reducible to 'knowing who' or 'knowing what', and what is more, 'knowing that' cannot take as its object any proposition whatsoever. In this sense faith is merely a kind of awareness which has as its object a limiting case, namely, the existence of unity in all. By its conceptual structure faith as superknowledge can be defined as a kind of *appearance,* because in the totality of forms *(logoi)* something appears which is more than the mere sum of forms, namely, *that* there is a unity in totality and *that* this unity is not describable in any discursive way. In this sense God is a limiting case for coherent thinking; this is why faith as *epignosis* is mystical.[7]

4.3 Conclusions

It is to be seen that some of the metalogical criteria of epistemic notions get a somewhat different emphasis in Christian Neo-Platonism than in Augustinian thinking. Firstly, as I have already said, the condition of truth for faith is accepted. This is similar to St. Augustine's criterion (1'). But the explanation is rather that faith as »superknowledge« implies a causal connection to its object.

On the other hand, it is clear that faith as »superknowledge« *(epignosis)* has nothing to do with ordinary scientific knowledge, because

---

[6] See Pseudo-Dionysios, *De divinis nominibus,* VII, 4.

[7] Compare Wittgenstein's thought according to which »Nicht *wie* die Welt ist, ist das Mystische, sondern *dass* sie ist« (*Tractatus* 6.44) and that the mystical concerns the *form* of all being (*Tractatus 6.3—6.4*). For Pseudo-Dionysios the unification with God is to be unified with the Idea of Oneness. *Cf. De divininis nominibus* VII, 2; XIII, 3; Gersh (1978) p. 268 (footnote 43).

scientific knowledge belongs to the »Aristotelian» katafatic category only and cannot correspondingly afford a real union between the knower and the known when the highest reality is at stake. It means that the condition of rational justification cannot be placed in the apofatic category in the sense of (2'), although it remains valid in the katafatic category in the sense of (2). Consequently, scientific knowledge and faith become more separated from each other than in Augustinian thinking. There cannot be simultaneous faith and scientific knowledge of God's »darkness», because faith is totally independent from discursive thinking.

We can also acquire a new outlook concerning the role of the so-called statistical modal theory. According to the classical conception genuine knowledge amounts to seeing the immutable forms or ideas, as it were, *always* i.e. in whatever context. In Neo-Platonism these forms are not immutable in the absolute sense, although they are immutable in the temporal sense; this is because they have emanated from the One. There is a difference between the classical and the Neo-Platonic understanding concerning how we could get into contact with the highest reality. The immutable forms of antiquity still have the status of perpetual truths for the Neo-Platonists; they can always and in every context be the objects of the intellect. However, according to the Neo-Platonists the highest reality, the One or God, cannot *always* be achieved by the intellect (because that would imply contradictions), but only in certain specific circumstances.

From the point of view of the knower, therefore, the highest reality has a similar status as propositions which are true in some circumstances and false in some others. The highest reality, of course, cannot lose its perpetual and immutable reality, but because it can be achieved only in some specific contexts, it is precisely faith that possesses also the conceptual structure of what the ordinary belief or opinion had in classical theory. Specifically this means that faith in this sense resembles the subjectivistic and contextual character of belief. On the other hand, faith, by being a causally and conceptually necessary condition for getting in contact with God, works for deeper understanding and is in this sense in accordance with the Augustinian programme. This, I think, very clearly shows the fluctuating nature of faith in Christian Neo-Platonism.

5. BOETHIUS AS THE MEDIATOR OF THE ARISTOTELEAN AND THE PLATONIC TRADITION

The difference between the Augustinian, Christian Neo-Platonic and Boethian epistemic logic is not very great, but there are some typical Aristotelean traits in the epistemic notions of the »last Roman». The main reason for his typical emphasis is the Neo-Platonic challenge consisting of an ontologisation of the meanings of predicate terms. The main confusion on this area was the following:

In some contexts a general term, like 'homo', cannot function as a name, e.g. when we say 'Socrates est homo', because we are predicating humanitas of Socrates. Sometimes, however, the name 'homo' was taken as referring to the same as 'humanitas', For example, in this connection Boethius said that 'humanitas' is the name of the class of men. But now it was easy to slip to think that a class, as *extension,* is as if being substituted for a property, as *intension.* This is because if we take 'humanitas' as a *name,* it cannot have any intension. But if the intension has taken the place of the extension, then it easy to take the very intension or concept *as extension.* In this way the term 'homo' could be understood as naming its own meaning (intension). This was the main idea in the socalled »two name theory» of the propositional meaning which had its roots already in Aristotle.[1]

5.1 Boethius' Ambivalence

The confusion which I mentioned above was apt to lead to *mentalistic*

---

[1] Aristotle, *Metaphysics* XII, 1071a, 1078b; II, 3, 998b; *Topics* IV, 6, 127a; *Categories* 11b—15b; Pinborg (1972) p. 38—42. One root of the confusion was to take some so-called 2. impositions (words referring to linguistic entities) for 1. impositions (words referring to extralinguistic entities) or for 1. intentions (mental words referring to extra-mental reality). See Chr. Knudsen, »Intentions and Impositions» *LMP* p. 484—485; W. and M. Kneale, *The Development of Logic.* Oxford 1966, p. 196—197.

semantics which, in turn, had its impact on the epistemic logic of Boethius (480—524). He follows Porphyrios by saying that we call mind that faculty of the soul by which we think of the eternal truths, and belief or opinion the faculty by which we think of universal conventions, and further perception or imagination the faculty by which we consider individuals.[2] We see here how the faculties of the soul reach different objects beginning from the highest. Because these objects are, at the same time, something mental, they come very close to mental acts themselves. This implies the familiar trend of antiquity: as mental acts the propositional attitudes of knowledge, belief and imagination seem to achieve their proper objects automatically. This is to accept (C.S) and (C.T).

In spite of the trend towards homogenizing belief and knowledge Boethius quite strongly separates them, too. The separation is built into his view of God's foreknowledge. Because God as atemporal being sees all truths at one and the same time, determinism seems to follow. This is not, however, the case according to Boethius, because there we have a decisive difference between the point of view of God and man. All truths, including contingent truths, are from the point of view of God objects of knowledge, not belief. Therefore, they are immutably true and determinate. But from the point of view of man they are as all contingent truths, i.e. their truth-value changes temporally. This means that the same contingent truths can be simultaneously both objects of knowledge and of belief, although in the former case they are considered by God, in the latter case by man.[3]

One could think that this, too, makes belief close to knowledge. However, Boethius is quite convinced that they are separate. His main idea is that we cannot rationally understand the notion of providence, because

---

[2] Cf. Boethius' commentary on Aristotle's *Prior Analytics, Aristoteles latinus,* III, Ed. L. Minio-Paluello, Leiden 1969, p. 310; compare Aristotle, *Categories* 12b 6—15, 4b 8, 14b 21; Nuchelmans, »The Semantics of Propositions«, *LMP* p. 198—199. Other discussion on Boethius' Platonism, see: Pinborg (1972) p. 40; M. Loux, *Substance and Attribute.* Dordrecht-Holland/Boston-USA/London-England 1978, p. 146—147; J. Owens, »Faith, Ideas, Illumination, and Experience«, *LMP* p. 444; Kneale (1966) p. 196—197; Liebschütz, »Boethius and the Legacy of Antiquity«, *LGEMP* p. 541; H. Chadwick, *Boethius.* The Consolations of Music, Logic, Theology, and Philosophy. Oxford 1981, 193.

[3] See *De consol.* V, 6, 1—17; V, 6, 2—48; II, 7, 17; Chadwick (1981) p. 214—217, 220—221.

we cannot by logic, i.e. by syllogistic reasoning, unite the notions of divine determinate providence and the mutual contingent truths of the sensual world. So, if there is a harmony between knowledge and belief or faith, we cannot know it. Therefore, knowledge and faith are *parallel;* they do not meet, except in relatively rare cases where reason can with the help of logic clarify some obscurities of faith.[4]

Boethius' epistemic logic seems to imply, then, the acceptance of the condition of truth for faith *via* the mentalistic semantics, parallelism of faith and knowledge *via* having the same truths as objects and by the absence of syllogistic reasoning and simultaneity of faith and knowledge *via* being known by God and believed by man.

5.2 The Certainty of Faith and the Tradition of Topics

Boethius realised very clearly that although the truths of faith are not demonstrated they have the status of axioms by being absolutely certain. We cannot »see» their truth, but we can »hear» it. In the Aristotelean tradition certainties were apodictic (necessary or intuitively evident) or topical (universally accepted) propositions.[5] Because in theology some of these certainties were not universally accepted truths and did not have any other guarantee than suggested divine revelation in some human minds, they had to be accepted by »hearing» the voice of those truthful authorities. Some support for this view came from the mentalistic semantics, mentioned above, because revelational truths were easily interpreted as being their own quarantee simply by being present in the mind. This was to accept, as I said, the criterion (C.T) in some sense. So, there were no difficulties for Boethius to come to his »Regula Prima»:

> The common conception of the soul is a proposition which everyone accepts after hearing it.[6]

---

[4] *De consol.* V, 3, 26: »Quid enim divina providentia humana opinione praestiterit, si uti homines incerta indicaret, quorum est incertus eventus?» Compare also *De consol.* III, M, 11; IV, 6, 1—13; V, 6, 28—30; *De fato* 30; *De differentiis topicis* II (*PL* 64, 1185B); Chadwick (1981) p. 220—221; S. Knuuttila, »Modal Logic», *LMP* p. 342.

[5] See *Topics* 101b10—35; 103b—20; 100a 18.

[6] *De hebdomadibus (PL* 64, 1316D): »Communis animi conceptio est enuntiatio, quam quisque probat auditam.» The term 'enuntiatio' was generally understood

Boethius' Regula was to be applied to the statements of faith. The certainties of faith are thus like topical certainties, because they have a similar conceptual status: on the one hand they are parallel to the ordinary hearsay beliefs, on the other hand they are absolutely certain principles like the »seen» scientific truths.

This view of Boethius was later reinforced and transmitted to Scholasticism. For example, Gilbert of Poitiers (1076—1154) thought that the axioms on which theology is based are »absolute» principles which are immutable and necessary. But, he says, whilst we come to the principles of other sciences inductively and intuitively, in theology it is faith itself which is the basis of axioms. Faith is, in other words, itself the guarantee of its truth: if somebody believes religiously, he also knows or is absolutely certain, i.s. the formula (4) will be accepted in some sense.[7]

This standpoint was also linked with the Aristotelean idea of inductive generalisation in the *Topics*. Theological axioms can be accepted if they meet with general acceptance. Theological truths are indeed necessary, but in order to be so, from the point of view of man, they have to be true in the temporal sense *»semper»*. This is fulfilled when they are always believed by »many» or all. A condition purporting to this is proposed in the famous principle of Vincent of Lerin: »quod ubique, quod semper, quod ab omnibus creditum est». When a theological proposition satisfies this condition it is necessary, certain and immutable. But this is based on a topical interpretation of theological axioms and on a statistical theory of modalities. In this way a bridge is built up

---

as meaning 'enuntiare mentaliter quod sic est' i.e. mental proposition. See Nuchelmans, »The Semantics of Propositions», *LMP* p. 199.

[7] Cf. the commentary of Gilbert to the *De Trinitate* of Boethius *(PL* 64, 1303B): »In caeteris facultatibus, in quibus semper consuetudini regulae generalitas atque necessitas accommodatur, non ratio fidem sed fides sequitur rationem. Et quoniam in temporalibus nihil est, quod mutabilitati non sit obnoxium, tota illorum consuetudini accommodata necessitas nutat. Nam in eis quidquid praedicatur vel esse vel non esse, quodam modo nec esse nec non esse necesse est. Non enim absolute necessarium est, cui nomen 'necessitas' sola consuetudo accommodat. In theologicis autem, ubi est veri nominis atque absoluta necessitas, non ratio fidem, sed fides praevenit rationem. In his enim non cognoscentes credimus, sed credentes cognoscimus. Nam absque rationum principiis fides concipit non modo illa, quibus intelligendis humanae rationes suppeditare non possunt, verum etiam illa quibus ipsae possunt esse principia.»

between the certainty of faith and the certainty of topical or »dialectical» (probable) beliefs.

We see, again, how the subjectivistic, contextual and relativistic nature of belief was linked with the objective, necessary and absolute nature of knowledge. Faith and knowledge are on a par as sources of knowledge. For that reason there is no more need to think that the objects of faith and knowledge are simultaneous only on the basis of being the objects of divine intellect. Because the topical certainties of believers have the same or almost the same cognitive value as the *(apodictic)* certainties of knowledge, there is no problem about the simultaneity of two *different* epistemic attitudes, instead there will be simultaneity in the sense of coalescence of faith and knowledge.

6. THE LOGIC OF FAITH ACCORDING TO ST. ANSELM OF CANTERBURY

As is generally known, St. Anselm (1033—1109) seems to make a distinction between the conceptual (or mental) and the real in his famous Ontological Argument. At the same time, however, he also seems to base his Argument on the interplay between what is thought and what exists. Therefore, we have to ask first: what are the mentalistic background presuppositions in St. Anselm's Argument?

It is also well known that St. Anselm was quite convinced that some propositions of faith can be rationally demonstrated. These propositions, then, seem to be simultaneous objects of faith and knowledge. Is this a factor which weakens St. Anselm's view of the epistemic status of faith? That will be our second question here.

6.1 On the presuppositions of the Ontological Argument

Elswhere I have tried to argue that St. Anselm's Ontological Argument can be viewed to say that God's existence is a kind of necessary thought; although it does not follow from this as such that God exists also outside the mind, St. Anselm had some modal theory reasons for not distinguishing very sharply, when speaking of God, between what is merely thought, what is real and what is necessary.[1] Therefore, the core of the Ontological Argument might lie in this ontological mixture. In another words, we could propose that the Anselmian claim is: we can move from the scope of an intensional operator, namely, from that of thinking, into the scope of the existential quantifier in such a way that the existence of God be demonstrated. This happens *via* true *understanding*.

---

[1] Explicitly St. Anselm seems to make this distinction when he says: »Aliud enim est rem esse in intellectu, aliud intelligere rem esse.» *Proslogion* II; Kirjavainen (1983) p. 100—103.

Schematically we could represent the main suggestions of St. Anselm's argument in the following way:

(7)   Tp ⊃ p   /*Proslogion* IV, the acceptance of the criterion (C.T) by illumination

(8)   p ⊃ Mp   /*Proslogion* II, the premiss that the actual is »greater» than the possible

(9)   Np ⊃ p   /*Proslogion* III

Because St. Anselm had a statistical interpretation for necessity he also, in a sense, was inclined to accept what can be formulated as follows:

(10)   p ⊃ Np

This formulation expresses the so-called »necessitas sequens» which is one of his three interpretations for necessity: coercion, necessary thought and consequent necessity.[2] The interpretation in question says that the true, when it is, is also the necessary.

Now we can easily see that there would be fatal consequences if we accepted (10) without restrictions, e.g. that everything that is thought is necessary and that all that is the case is equal to necessity. Therefore, we have to ask: if St. Anselm did really accept (10) in some sense, what was involved? An answer would be that St. Anselm did not make a sharp distinction between *necessitas cogitationis* and *necessitas sequens*.

In answering we have to remind ourselves of two points: Firstly, because St. Anselm had adopted the statistical modal theory he thought that what is necessary is something which is *always*. Secondly, because he thought that it is sufficient merely to think of an object which no greater could be thought of, in order to grasp it, one then automatically grasps it as something which is always i.e. necessarily.

Beginning from this latter point we might sketch out an implicit

---

[2] The other two necessities are *necessitas coactionis* and *necessitas cogitationis*. Cf. *Cur Deus homo*, II, 17: »... et est necessitas sequens, quam res facit. ... sequens vero et quae nihil efficit sed fit, est cum dico te ex necessitate loqui, quia loqueris» *Ibid:* »Omnis necessitas est aut coactio aut prohibitio.» *Ibid:* »Cum ... dicimus aliquid necesse esse aut non esse in deo, non intelligitur quod sit in illo necessitas aut cogens aut prohibens.» *Proslogion* II: »Et quidem quidquid est aliud praeter te solum, potest cogitari non esse. Solus igitur verissime omnium, et ideo maximae omnium habes esse...» *Proslogion* XXII: »Tu vero es quod es, quia quidquid aliquando aut aliquo modo es, hoc totus et semper es... nec potes cogitari aliquando non esse.»

inference from thinking to necessary existence. According to it one first takes as an object of thinking precisely *that instance* which satisfies the condition (8) and which no greater could be thought of; one then substitutes it for p. Formally it would be something like

(**)   Tp ⊃ p, p/p ⊃ Mp, p/a

which means that if one thinks that p, then in only one substitution instance of p can one think of an object which no greater could be thought of. But *this* one and only substitution instance, when it is, and as soon as it is thought of, is necessary. If not existing, this instance would not be the one of which no greater could be thought of *(Proslogion* XV). Therefore,

(***)   a/p, p ⊃ Mp/p, p ⊃ Np,

which says that this specific object is something which is always i.e. exists necessarily. By taking these substitution instances as intermediary links there would be an inference from 'Tp' to 'Np'.

This is perhaps a slightly different way of seeing the ontological opacity of St. Anselm's Ontological Argument than to say that he handled existence as a predicate. Our way of seeing the situation relies on the hypothesis that, in the last analysis, God's existence in St. Anselm's argument is kept in the scope of intensional operator all the time, namely, the move is not made from thinking into existence as such but from one intensional operator (thinking) into the scope of another intensional operator, namely that of necessity. This can be put forwards by saying, somewhat roughly, that in order to exist God has to be thought of as the greatest possible object of *thought* which, of course, includes necessary existence.

What does this tell us? Well, first of all that St. Anselm's Argument had a kind of mentalistic background to it. He joined to the Augustinian tradition and took into account a possibility having at least some knowledge of reality with the help of mere rational and a *priori* analysis of the meaning of terms. 'God's existence' is such a term. Accordingly, there will always be room for the interrelationship of faith and knowledge, because a part of faith is simultaneously also known. But does this imply a weakening of the epistemic status of faith?

6.2 The Strengthening of Metalogical Duality

During St. Anselm's time it was widely approved that the truths of faith as premises were independent from the rational premises from which they might be deducible.[3] However, for St. Anselm it was important to hold on to the view of rational explication of the truths of faith in the Augustinian manner, because, according to him, it was man's task as a rational being to *reconstruct* afterwards a rational explication of what was previously believed by faith. This, of course, is to stick to the *fides quaerens intellectum* programme.[4]

There are, however, relatively few such truths of faith of which we can actually have a rational explication. This means that according to St. Anselm religious faith becomes to some extent *autonomous*. The autonomy is specifically based on the certainty which the truths of faith have. These truths might be even more certain than the rational premisses. But then the epistemic situation becomes preposterous: the truths of faith might be deducible as consequences from the premises which were less certain than those truths themselves.[5]

This standpoint led St. Anselm to distinguish between (in our sense) subjective and objective certainty. From this distinction we derive the role of rational explication for the truths of faith: it might support the *subjective* certainty of faith in some individual person, although it cannot increase the *objective* certainty of those truths. Therefore, revelational truths are best considered as *possible rational consequences*. There are some truths of faith which are such that we might have simultaneous objective certainty about them by knowing them to be revelational and we also might have a kind of rational subjective certainty by having them rationally demonstrated. The demonstration cannot increase the objec-

---

[3] See e.g. John of Salisbury, *Metalogicon,* 649B, 650B: »Habet et religio quaelibet principia sua, quae aut ratio communis aut pietas persuavit.»

[4] Cf. *Proslogion,* Proemium: This view is quite widely accepted among scholars, though it is not the only one. See e.g. H. Liebschütz, »Anselm of Canterbury: The Philosophical Interpretation of Faith», *LGEMP,* p. 629; M. J. Charlesworth, *St. Anselms Proslogion.* (Philosophical Commentary) Oxford 1965, p. 33—34, 36; G. Leff, *Medieval Thought.* London 1958, p. 99; D. P. Henry, *Medieval Logic and Metaphysics.* London 1972, p. 106.

[5] St. Anselm makes a distinction between 'having necessary causes' and 'being deducible'. All truths of faith have necessary causes of which only some are deducible. See Charlesworth (1965) p. 35—36.

tive certainty, therefore, one's cognitive obligation to the truths of faith does not depend on demonstration.[6]

Consequently, there might be simultaneously a religious and a cognitive obligation to believe these truths. But this does not mean that faith and knowledge were, according to St. Anselm, similar epistemic notions. Because the certainty of faith and the certainty of knowledge belong to different species there is a preliminary metalogical gap between faith and knowledge. This insinuates of a certain differentiation in the epistemic roles of faith and knowledge. And, of course, St. Anselm would not say that by having faith one always simultaneously knows something; this can only be done if one has rationally demonstrated that one also knows the truths of faith.

---

[6] See *Proslogion,* XIV: »Nam si non invenisti deum tuum: quomodo est ille hoc quod invenisti, et quod illum tam certa veritate et certitudine intellexisti?» (Objective certainties) »Quid puritatis, quid simplicitatis, quid certitudinis et splendoris ibi est!» Our usage of the terms 'objective' and 'subjective' is not the same as in the Middle Ages.

7. THE METAPHYSICS OF KNOWING BEFORE ST. THOMAS AQUINAS

From the early Middle Ages to the period of Scholasticism theological thinkers had to face the growing problem of how to systematize the doctrinal heritage. This situation was to lead to the development of theological methodology and at last to what is usually called »scholastic method». The development had different sources: partly it arose from the problematics concerning the axiomatic-deductive ideal of Aristotelean science, partly from the problems concerning the suitable topical premisses for theological thinking, and partly from the methodological discussions of *artes liberales.*[1]

As the result, the scholastic method included generally syllogistic logic added with the suitable principles, namely profane topical premisses + theological topical premisses *(loci regulaeque).* Pierre Abelard (1079—1142) in his book *Sic et non* and Petrus Lombardus (1095—1164) in his book *Libri quattuor sententiarum* had an essential influence for this development of the scholastic method.[2]

The scholastic science had, however, to overcome more difficult problems than the problems of finding suitable methodological rules for handling the theological material. They had to ask: Could we have a genuine scientific knowledge concerning the objects of theology? If the logic to be used in theology is correct, what is to be said of the epistemological status of those objects?

Augustinian thinkers, Robert Grosseteste (1175—1253), William of Auxerre (1165—1230), William of Auvergne (1175—1249), St. Albert the Great (1193—1280), Roger Bacon (1214—1292) and St. Bonaventura (1221—1274), tried to solve the problem of the epistemological status of

---

[1] See e.g. Martin Grabmann, *Die Geschichte der scholastischen Methode.* Freiburg im Breisgau 1911; Albert Lang, *Die theologische Prinzipienlehre der mittelalterlichen Scholastik.* Freiburg — Basel — Wien 1964.

[2] Cf. Pinborg (1972) p. 21—29; Lang (1964) Parts I—III.

theological premisses on the lines of a double aspect theory. Theological *loci* concern entities which are in a way on a par with natural *genera* and metaphysical categories. The propositions speaking of these entities, however, consist of terms which refer to contingent matters e.g. historical events or persons. How can such a proposition be contingent and, at the same time, universally valid without being necessary? During the discussion, step by step, the double aspect theory emerged and reached its culmination in St. Bonaventura's *subalternation* theory.

7.1 Objects of knowledge and faith

The Augustinian Franciscans generally took their point of departure from the thought that in some way theological but contingent propositions must have an eternal object. The background of this view was the semantic discussion concerning the objects of faith. St. Augustine in his commentary to St. John had said that the objects of faith are the same to those who have been before Christ and to those who come after him.[3] This led e.g. Peter Lombard and Hugo St. Victor to put the question: If the articles of faith are the same to the *antiqui* as well as to the *moderni,* how can we explain the identity of the articles if their formulation is different?

There were two types of semantic theories that arose as alleged answers: according to the first type the objects of faith are things *(res)* or named entities *(incomplexa),* according to the second type they are propositions *(complexa).* In res-theories the identity of the object of faith was preserved by saying that God is a simple object, that all virtues presuppose the same object and that propositions cannot be the causes of opinions *(enuntiabilia).* Furthermore, if we take the proposition 'Christ suffers' as an object of faith, then no one now living can orthodoxically believe it, because the proposition is true only at the moment Christ suffers.[4] As a counterargument it was stated that if the object of faith is an atemporal *res,* say 'the incarnation of Christ' then there is no difference between those who believe it to have happened and those who heretics who

---

[3] *In Johannis Evangelium Tractatus* XLV, 9 *(CC,* vol. XXXVI).

[4] The argument is based on the Aristotelean statistical presupposition according to which propositions are temporally tied to the moment of expression. See *De anima* 430b; *Categories* 4a 22.

still wait for it to happen. One solution was offered by saying that the objects of faith are the acts of believing. But this was opposed by the Provost of Cremona. We could not, he says, correctly analyse the saying 'believe something', because it would be identical with 'believe (the act of) believing'.[5]

All *complexum*-theories had to face the problem of postulating a special world between the mental and the real, the world of *enuntiabilia* or *dicta*. It is demonstrably very difficult to define the identity conditions of these *enuntiabilia* in such a way that they would not be temporally vulnerable or that they would not become *res*. The major Franciscan effort was to try to make them eternal.[6] The object of faith is to be found in *esse essentiae,* which is identical with the eternal image in God's thought independently from *esse existentiae,* which is the actually existing thing. If we are considering an object of religious belief, say a contingent proposition that Christ is incarnated, then the semantics of this proposition can be understood in a double way: explicitly as standing for a linguistic expression, implicitly as standing for a thing *(res)*. The former alternative (explicit faith) concerns something mutable, temporally specifiable, a contingent proposition whose truth value changes, the latter (implicit faith) something immutable which could be characterised e.g. by a passive-infinitive construction *'Christum incarnari'*.[7] We see here clearly the tendency of linking faith with the immutable eternal reality, but at the risk of loosing the propositional character of faith.

7.2 Illumination and Certainty

One of the most central questions in this period concerns the function

[5] See Nuchelmans (1973) p. 180; similar point is made by William Auxerre in *Summa aurea* III, 2, cap.2, q.2.

[6] See Nuchelmans *LMP* 202—203; Nuchelmans, *Theories of the Proposition. Ancient and medieval conceptions of the bearers of truth and falsity.* North-Holland Linguistic Series, Eds. S.C. Dik and J.G. Kooij, Amsterdam — London 1973, p. 182—185.

[7] St. Bonaventura describes different semantic theories in his commentary to sentences. See *In quattuor libros sententiarum* III, dist. 24, q. 3, art. 1. Cf. St. Augustine, *In Johannis Evangelium tractatus* XLV, 9 *(CC* vol XXXVI). Later this problem was acutely discussed under the heading »*Utrum haec sit vera: homo est animal, nullo homine existente*«. See Ferdinand van Steenberghen, *Die Philosophie im 13. Jahrhundert*. München — Paderborn — Wien 1977, p. 443.

of illumination. The positions taken by two eminent contemporary representatives, Robert Grosseteste and William Auxerre, were somewhat different. We shall look at them each in turn.

Grosseteste's main point on faith was that it is based on authoritative knowledge and is dependent on moral effort. There are three sources of knowledge: authority, deductive reasoning and experience. But there is one unshakable criterion of knowledge: illumination. The most certain type of knowing is mathematics, because the divine light containing the substantial forms of things obeys geometrical principles. Therefore, knowing a truth is tantamount to thinking in conformity with the divine light i.e. mathematics.[8] But knowledge of the world, even metaphysical knowledge, is less certain than pure mathematics, since man has lapsed because of the sins of the flesh. Therefore, man needs moral effort, which would purify his soul so that he may accurately see everything in the divine light.[9]

Grosseteste was thus supporting a thesis according to which being revealed guarantees objective (ontological) certainty. But this can also be understood the other way around, namely, that what is absolutely certain is illuminated. So he thinks that when somebody considers a revealed proposition he knows at the same time that he knows that proposition. Such a certain proposition could not be false, because being illuminated it is in conformity with God's thinking.[10] Therefore, to be revealed is to be illuminated i.e. felt or seen by the soul to be true. This means that illumination is a kind of two-way light (primary i.e. *lux* and reflected i.e. *lumen);* an ontological as well as an epistemic *guarantee*

---

[8] »... for all causes of natural effects must be expressed by means of lines, angles and figures.» Grosseteste, *De Lineis, Angulis et Figuris.* Ed. L. Baur 1912, p. 59—60 (cit. acc. to A. A. Maurer, C.S.B., *Medieval Philosophy* New York 1968, p. 120—121).

[9] »... nulla conscipitur veritas nisi in luce summae veritatis... immundi multi summam veritatem vident (in conjunctione... rebus veris) et multi eorum nec percipiunt se videre eam aliquo modo ... Mundicores vero et perfecte purgati ipsam lucem in se conscipiunt... Nemo est igitur, qui verum aliquid novit, qui non aut scienter aut ignoranter etiam ipsam summam veritatem aliquo modo novit.» *De Veritate.* Ed. L. Baur 1912, p. 138.3—21 (cit. acc. to E. Serene, »Demonstrative science», *LMP* p. 502).

[10] »... veritas cuiscunque est eius conformitas rationi suae in aeterno Verbo.» Grosseteste, *Commentaria in Libros Posteriorum Analyticorum Aristotelis* by E. Serene, *LMP* p. 502.

of truth. So, basically authoritative propositions become cognitively obligatory by being accepted as premises for deductive reasoning. But because the truths of faith are contingent their certainty in the soul does not always stand; a specific act of God *(gratia infusa)* is therefore needed as well as man's own moral effort.[11]

We might conclude, firstly, that Grosseteste had a certain purpose for illumination in that it is a peculiar justification condition both for knowledge and faith. As soon as somebody knows something he also touches the highest truth which, in turn, makes him know that he knows. It follows that by faith man knows certain things. Secondly, Grosseteste does not think that there would be any need for reducing the one into the other; therefore the programme *fides quaerens intellectum* is alien to him. All certainty is based on the same source and all certainty, be it doxastic or epistemic, is of the same order. Consequently and thirdly, there might be simultaneous knowledge and faith, because they do not differ metalogically, but only concerning the object.

There is then a certain emerging theory of double illumination. But there is also the question of how, in the last analysis, one is to separate these two illuminations from each other. This question was answered by William Auxerre.

7.3 The function — object duality

William Auxerre was the first to distinguish between things whose essencies can be epistemically reached with the help of existing objects (i.e. *esse existentiae)* and things which we cannot so reach. All natural knowledge belongs to the first category, the principles of faith and science belong to the second. Therefore, we need divine illumination only in this second area. Natural comprehension does not need any supernatural illumination, because the causal factor producing forms or ideas in the soul is not God's thinking, but, on Aristotelean lines, the so-called *active intellect* abstracting the forms from material objects for the passive or potential intellect.[12]

---

[11] See Serene's explication of the statistical character of the truth of premises in *LMP* p. 503, note 27.

[12] On active and passive intellect see Aristotle, *De anima* III, 5, 430a24; Alexander Aphrodisias, *De anima* 81, 24—25; Z. Kuksewicz, »The Potential and Agent Intellect«, *LMP* p. 595—596.

In the meeting of the Augustinian and Aristotelean metaphysics of knowing a new phase developed concerning the problem of illumination. According to the Augustinian tradition the intellect can be directed by double illumination either to heavenly or to sensual things. This distinction was now to be united with the Aristotelean distinction between *intellectus* and *ratio* in the first place and 'active' and 'passive' intellect in the second place. The first link was not very problematic, because the directedness upwards could simply be understood as *intellectus (nous)* and directedness downwards as *ratio*.

The second link was much harder. According to the Aristotelean view the model case of knowledge occurs when the active intellect abstracts from the sensible things their conceptually essential and immutable traits; in addition, we can have knowledge only of things of which there are exemplars in the world. This model case of knowledge, however, is bound to belong, according to the Augustinian conception, to the »lower» level. Therefore, abstracted natural knowledge *(comprehensio)* is only »lower» knowledge. Two problems arise: (1) How do we gain the »higher» knowledge? (2) In which sense can the »lower» knowledge be certain and necessary?

There were many solutions to these questions. According to William Auvergne there is no need for a separate active intellect as an outside factor, because the passive (material) intellect as soul is enough for producing the species without any outside factor. Therefore, there is no place for any illumination either, because the truth is grasped by thinking which is the soul's proper function. But as a reminiscence of an illumination Auvergne says that the soul has two parts: abstractive and »angelic». The latter is a substitute of illumination.[13]

Albert The Great thought that external objects cannot produce forms in the intellect; the producer must be the active intellect, which is the essence *(esse)* of the soul, and participating in God's own intellect, the light whereby we understand. But, St. Albert wants to say, the forms in the mind are not, however, entities separated from individual things. The forms in the mind are not beings, but *properties* which include individual things. This sounds very Aristotelian, but there is a kind of

---

[13] William Auvergne, *De Anima* VII, 3, 206b *(Opera omnia,* Orleans and Paris 1674 reprinted by Minerva 1963): J. Owens, »Faith, Ideas, Illumination, and Experience», *LMP* p. 445—447.

compromise with Augustinian thinking, too. The light of natural reason must be subordinated to the »uncreated light», which has the power of illuminating the soul independently of the sensual world.[14]

Roger Bacon also thought that the forms are not conditions of being, but of knowing. The soul is largely identical with the passive intellect, but through the Fall it has lost its divine ideas now being almost totally a *tabula rasa*. The soul acquires forms through the active intellect which, is universal and common to all men. In order to gain knowledge of the sensual world the passive intellect needs illumination which regenerates corrupted innate ideas. Bacon thinks that the forms produced by the active intellect are in a way measures of grasping the outside world. Illumination is thus the basic causal factor in the cognitive process, a factor which provides the human mind with *a priori* tools for handling phenomena.[15]

In all these solutions faith and knowledge tend to coincide, because in both the function of illumination is nearly the same, namely, that of the active intellect illuminating the mind. But then the core of the problem lies in the fact that the objects of faith and knowledge are not the same, because in the former case the objects are from »above» and in the latter case from »below». Therefore, there cannot be total parity between faith and knowledge. We shall see what St. Bonaventura has to say on this matter.

7.4 St. Bonaventura

St. Bonaventura, like most other Franciscan thinkers, suggested an implicit link between man's efforts to know and to live a virtuous life. Therefore, one of his background suppositions was that there is a higher knowledge than ordinary earthly knowledge, which is hardly anything more than opinion. One of the roots of this view was semantic, namely, that it is purely a contingent matter whether a concept or the meaning of a term is true of the world. This Stoic and Augustinian theory was entirely contrary to the Aristotelean semantics according to which the relation between a concept and the world is a necessary one, and conse-

---

[14] St. Albert says that although man's intellect is united with the body it is not excluded from the capacity of the »pure light of understanding of intelligible objects». See *Summa Theologiae* II, 14, 2; I, 15, 3; *De Intellectu et Intelligibili* I, 1, 6; II, 5.

[15] See *Quaestiones supra libros quatuor Physicorum,* vol. 8 p. 31; *Opus majus,* II, 5; Owens *LMP* p. 449; Kuksewicz *LMP* p. 598—600.

quently true of the world. According to Stoics there is no such necessity concerning the *lekta* i.e. meanings of terms.[16]

The Augustinian view had epistemological import, too. We can, thought St. Bonaventura, achieve concepts by abstraction from sensual things, but this Aristotelean formation of concepts does not lead any further than to likenesses or opinions. Therefore, there is no absolute certainty or necessity in the natural comprehension of things effected by the active and passive intellect. The real correspondence holds for the relation between the images of the soul and immutable divine ideas. Truth as the correspondence relation between human and divine intellect is the proper concern of higher knowledge.[17]

The object of faith and knowledge, says St. Bonaventura, is not a thing *(res),* but a *complexum* or *enuntiabile.* The *enuntiabile* is twofold: either temporally specifiable or temporally indeterminate like *'Christum incarnari'.* Epistemologically this indeterminate *enuntiabile* is identical with the illuminated form i.e. *impressio,* which in turn is quite a different thing from the abstracted form, this latter being also the result of a kind of illumination, namely, of that for producing an intelligible species.[18] These two forms correspond to the famous distinction of St. Bonaventura: *»supra et infra».*[19] Our true knowledge is from above as compared to the abstracted knowledge of the exemplars in the world.[20]

Certain important consequences follow: firstly, knowledge and faith can have the same object at the same time, namely, the same *enuntiabile,*

---

[16] See Pinborg (1972) p. 30—31.

[17] *In Sent.* II, 24, 1, 2, 4; II, 39, 1, 2; *De scientia Christi* IV; *De Mysterio Trinitatis* I, 1; *Itinerarium mentis in Deum* III, 1; Maurer (1968) p. 149—150.

[18] *In Sent.* I, 3, 1, ad 5: »Deus est praesens ipsi animae et omni intellectui per veritatem; ... dum cognoscitur ab intellectu, intellectus informantur quadam notitia, quae est velut similitudo quedam non abstracta, sed impressa»; *In Sent.* II, 3, 2, 2, 2: »Divina lux propter sui eminentiam est inaccessibilis viribus omnis naturae creatae; et ideo per quandam benignitatis *condescensionem* facit se cognosci...» Attempts have been made to formulate indeterminate *enuntiabilia* in such a way that the speaker is in a temporally indifferent position. See Nuchelmans *LMP* p. 203.

[19] *In Sent.* III, 24, 3, 1: »... sic nihil impedit, unum et idem secundum et alium cognoscendi modum esse infra et supra; et ita scitum et creditum.

[20] The point made here by St. Bonaventura is slightly different from that made by Aristotle, who said that one cannot know and believe the same thing at the same time, because the former is necessary and the latter contingent. See *Anal. post.* I, 33, 89a 18—25.

but seen as if from a different angle, from above and from below.[21] We could say that St. Bonaventura does not offer a satisfactory answer here. He only seems to say that if two cognitive faculties do have the same object then they are similar and compatible. On the other hand, he also says that in that case these faculties are two different modes *(modum)* and thus somewhat contrary to each other.

Secondly, we have here a full-fledged double aspect theory. In a certain sense faith is knowledge, because it is on a par with the true knowledge coming from illumination, and containing within itself absolute certainty. But, on the other hand, faith is not knowledge, because faith is always based on authority and higher illumination, not on rational demonstrative argument. These two determinations »distract in opposite directions». If somebody believes something by faith then he knows that he knows this something to be true, because it would be impossible for this something to be false. The ontological certainty is guaranteed by illumination.[22] On the other hand, if somebody believes something by faith then he might or might not have the ordinary knowledge of it. He might merely believe it by faith, but he might also have demonstrative knowledge of it. Therefore, in the former sense faith is a species of knowledge being always based on illumination and infallible authority, in the latter sense faith has a relatively independent status, because it is not ordinary knowledge.

Thirdly, we see that because higher knowledge converges upon faith, then what we believe here by faith the angels and the blessed know in the realms of higher knowledge. Therefore, there is a *subalternative* relation between these two species of knowing.

As it is with a subalternate science, whenever it is deficient it is drawn back to the certainty of the subaltering science which has a greater certainty. Similarly, when a magister is short of the rational certainty he runs back to

[21] *In Sent.* III, 24, 3, 1: »unde aliquis credens, Deum esse unum, creatorem omnium, si ex rationibus necessariis incipiat idem nosse, non propter hoc desinit fidem habere.«

[22] *In Sent.,* Prooemium q. 2, ad 4: »Quoniam igitur sacra Scriptura est de credibili ut credibili, hic est de credibili ut facto intelligibili, et haec determinatio distrahit. Nam quod credimus debemus auctoritati et quod intelligimus rationi. Hinc est quod sicut alius modus certitudinis est in scientia superiori et inferiori, ita alius modus certitudinis est in Sacra Scriptura et alius in hoc libro, et ideo alius modus procedendi.«

the certainty of the authority of Sacred Scripture which has certainty exceeding the certainty of reason.[23]

The double aspect theory of St. Bonaventura, then, reflects a culmination of the Augustinian programme of *fides quaerens intellectum* by tending to assimilate the metalogical power of religious faith with that of knowledge.

---

[23] *Ibid.,* Prooemium 2, ad 4: »Et sicut scientia subalternata, ubi deficit, redit ad certitudinem scientiae subalternantis, quae maior est; sic etiam, cum Magistro deficit certitudo rationis, recurrit ad auctoritatis certitudinem sacrae Scripturae, quae excedit omnem certitudinem rationis.« Compare Prooemium 1, ad 5—6: »Credibile enim, secundum quod habet in se rationem primae veritatis, cui fides assentit propter se et super omnia, pertinet ad doctrinam sacrae Scripturae, ... sed secundum quod supra rationem veritatis et auctoritatis addit rationem probabilitatis, pertinet ad considerationem praesentis libri, in quo ponantur rationes probantes fidem nostram.«

8. THE CERTAINTY OF FAITH AND EPISTEMIC LOGIC ACCORDING TO ST. THOMAS AQUINAS

We have recently seen how the tendency of placing the objects of faith on the most valuable level of reality led to an emphasis on assimilating faith to knowledge. However, at the dawn of High Scholasticism it was quite clear that faith is something other than knowledge, or even rational belief. The Franciscan solution to this ambivalence, the double aspect theory, did not quite satisfy St. Thomas's Aristotelian standards. He tried to offer a solution of his own. But did he invent something new, or did he remain within the framework of antique presuppositions? Did he accept, firstly, what we have called *the implicit teleology,* and secondly, what we have called *the statistical modal theory?* According to the former, epistemic notions imply a conceptual connection to an end, according to the latter, knowledge implies necessity, which is to be understood by speaking of what always is i.e. immutably and eternally.

8.1 The problems of St. Thomas

St. Thomas discusses the nature of epistemic and doxastic notions in *Summa* (*PP,* 84—89; *PS,* 55, 62; *SS,* 1—7), and in *Quaestiones disputatae* (mainly *De veritate,* q. 14).[1] Many scholars have been puzzled by two apparently incompatible statements of St. Thomas. He seems to think that faith and knowledge are excludingly separate, but also that faith is a kind of knowledge: »the same person cannot have scientific knowledge and faith of the same thing» and »the human intellect cannot know high-

---

[1] There are some differences between the *Summa* and *De veritate,* but I am not going to analyse them, because they are of no importance considering the fact that *Summa* was written almost fifteen years later than *De veritate.* The most important articles in *De veritate* are 1 (»What is believing?») and 2 (»What is faith?») and in *SS* the question 1 (»The object of faith») and 2 (»The inner act of faith»).

er intelligibles, unless it is completed by some stronger light, like the light of faith».[2]

If we take the first statement at its face value, it seems to imply the rejection of the »corner stone of epistemic logic»[3], namely, rejecting the Platonic principle

$$(3) \qquad K_a p \supset B_a p,$$

i.e. belief cannot be a conceptual ingredient of knowing. This has surprised some scholars because St. Thomas seems to think, like St. Augustine, that if somebody believes something by faith then this something is true, namely,

$$(1') \qquad B^{faith}_a p \supset p,$$

i.e. faith is such a strong belief that it conceptually implies the metalogical criterion of truth, thus it converges upon knowledge. On the basis of this some scholars have been inclined to maintain that St. Thomas accepted the view that faith is a supernatural species of knowledge.[4]

Timothy Potts has sought an explanation in another direction.[5] »His view seems to be», says Potts, »that the will is involved in belief in the following way: I believe that p when I accept that p *as means to some end* which I want to attain.» (Potts' italics) This proposal, however, causes immediate difficulties. Is it meant that merely 'believing that p' is the means or that 'the state of affairs that p' is the means? What does 'means' here refer to — to the act (or attitude) of believing or to a state of affairs? Either interpretation seems very problematic.

---

[2] *SS,* 2, 4, ad 2: ». . . de eodem non potest esse scientia et fides apud eumdem. Sed id quod est ab uno scitum potest esse ab alio creditum,» *SS,* 1, 5: »Non autem est possibile quod idem ab eodem sit visum et creditum, sicut supra dictum est. Unde etiam impossibile est quod ab eodem idem sit scitum et creditum.» *PS,* 109, 1: »Altiora vero intelligibilia intellectus humanus cognoscere non potest, nisi fortiori lumine perficiatur, sicut lumine fidei.»

[3] See Lenzen (1978) p. 27.

[4] See especially the so-called *nouvelle theologie* school: Henri de Lubac, *Surnaturel*. Etudes historiques. Paris 1946; Joseph Maréchal, Le point de depart de la métaphysique V, *Le thomisme devant la philosophie critique*. 2. édition, Bruxelles 1947; Karl Rahner, *Hörer des Wortes*. Zur Grundlegung einer Religionsphilosophie. München 1941.

[5] T. Potts, »Aquinas on Belief and Faith», *Inquiries into Medieval Philosophy.* A Collection in Honor of Francis P. Clarke. Westport, Connecticut 1971, p. 7.

Our main question is whether St. Thomas really understood faith and knowledge as mutually exclusive. This question entails many minor questions. We must consider: (1) What is the relationship between the acts of mind and the objects of those acts? (2) How did St. Thomas approach the Platonic-Aristotelean view that for it to be a different mental faculty amounts to it being a different object? (3) Did he see the objects of faith as propositions or things? (4) What is the role of knowledge by acquaintance in St. Thomas' epistemic thought? (5) Is it possible to realise the object of faith by believing? (6) What explanatory value do the implicit and explicit teleology as well as the statistical modal theory have in these connections?

8.2 The distinctions of the intellect

According to St. Thomas, human understanding *(intellectus)* can be described by distinguishing between 'think that' and 'think something'. The former refers to the relation between understanding and some proposition and is called the complex understanding *(intellectus complex)*, being divisible into two parts: composition and division. The latter St. Thomas calls the intellect which understands the indivisibles *(intelligentia indivisibilium);* normally this intellect is expressed by all those linguistic expressions which have the form 'a has in mind some . . .' referring to some individual substance.[6]

St. Thomas seems to think that somehow the latter understanding is more basic, which would mean that knowledge by acquaintance would be primary and that knowledge and belief as propositional attitudes were secondary.[7]

There is also another trait that causes some puzzlement. St. Thomas does not make a very effective distinction between propositional attitudes and propositional acts. »Composition» and »division» are acts as well as attitudes. This is partly explained by the distinction between the first

---

[6] Cf. *SS,* 83, 1; *PP,* 16, 2; *PP* 85, 5; *De veritate* 14, 1; A. Kenny, *Aquinas.* Oxford 1980, p. 62—65; Edouard-Henri Wéber, »Les discussions de 1270 a l'université de Paris et leur influence sur la pensée philosophique de S. Thomas d'Aquin», *Die Auseinandersetzungen an der Pariser Universtät im XIII. Jahrhundert.* Ed. A. Zimmermann, Miscellanea medievalia, Band 10, Berlin — New York 1976, p. 290—291.

[7] Because St. Thomas mostly uses the pronoun 'aliquid' as a variable it is not always clear whether he means a proposition or a thing (res).

and the second actuality: first actualities are possibilities, because they are habits, second actualities are temporally and locally specifiable acts. The ontological status of habits and acts was difficult to define for St. Thomas,[8] but this need not bother us here, because we are not interpreting St. Thomas' ontological commitments when we use expressions like 'B$_a$p' for his epistemic notions. It only needs to be remembered that as propositional attitudes knowledge and belief are primarily habits (1. actualities), as acts they are assents (2. actualities).

8.3 The looseness of assent

The most fundamental characterizing factor in epistemic and doxastic attitudes is, according to St. Thomas, the assent, which is thus the basic mental act in this connection. With the help of assent he firstly illustrates doubting.

$$(D) \qquad D_a p = \; \sim A_a p \; \& \; \sim A_a \sim p^9$$

According to the illustration a person doubts the proposition p when he neither assents to it nor to its negation. Generally St. Thomas thinks that a person must have some evidence or reason for his assenting. Therefore, the withdrawing from assent is conceptually linked with the fact that evidence does not support p more than its negation.

There is one immediate worry here. It follows from (D) that $D_a p$ and $D_a \sim p$ are equivalent and symmetrical. This, however, is only a kind of an illusion. If somebody e.g. doubts whether the third world war will begin tomorrow, it is not the same as doubting whether the third world war will begin sometime later in the future, although this latter state of

---

[8] If the intellect is the substantial form of the soul then it seems difficult to say that it consists of acts which are particular. If, on the other hand, the intellect is something habitual then it seems to be merely potential. Therefore, St. Thomas says that: »habitus quodammodo est medium inter potentiam puram et purum actum». *PP* 87, 2. Cf. the conflict between St. Thomas and St. Bonaventura and Siger of Brabant; Wéber (1976) p. 292—316; Kenny (1980) p. 65—66.

[9] See *De ver.* 14, 1: ». . . dubitans non habet assensum, cum non inhaereat uni parti magis quam alteri». Compare *SS* 1, 4—5; 2, 1; *PP* 84, 5. Of doubting and certainty see *SS,* 4, 8 ob 1: »Dubitatio enim opponitur certitudini; unde videtur illud esse certius quod minus potest habere de dubitatione,»; 3 *Sent.* 17, 1, 4c: ». . . principaliter (dubitatio) significat motum rationis supra utramque partem contradictionis cum formidine determinandi,».

affairs is implied by $D_a \sim p$. It is interesting that St. Thomas is probably aware of the intensional nature of the operator 'D', because he tries to characterize it as expressing different concepts. We will return to this again shortly».

Weak belief or opinion is characterized as follows

(O) $O_a p = A_a p \ \& \ D_a \sim p.$

It is conspicuous that St. Thomas deviates here from Plato and Aristotle, because according to him opinare $\neq$ credere. The reason is that he understands assent as an act which automatically grasps the alternative which of the two contradictories is the more probable one. Grasping this alternative does not, however, totally nullify the possibility of the contradictory. But this idea is logically suspect, because it implies the following inconsistency. If weak belief includes doubt and doubt is defined by (D), then: because $O_a p$ implies $D_a \sim p$ and because from $D_a \sim p$ it follows the formula $\sim A_a p$ then, if from (O) it follows $A_a p$, then (O) implies both $A_a p$ and $\sim A_a p$.

This inconsistency is illuminating because it is a consequence of the difficulties in the most profound presuppositions in St. Thomas' epistemic thought. One of the roots of the difficulties is, I think, the following. The difference between doubt and opinion is characterized as a change from a situation where there is no acceptance of a proposition to a situation where there *begins* to be some acceptance of a proposition. This means that the intellect which did not have any object now begins to have one, therefore, there is first a change among the objects which the soul has a grasp of. But if the attitude itself also changes along with the object it is nothing else than conceptually tied with the object. This has been, I think, the secret root of St. Thomas' purposes when he included a contradiction ($A_a p \ \& \ \sim A_a p$) in his characterization of opinion: he simply presupposed that the attitude of opinion, is *itself a kind of a change*.[10]

This explanation gains some support from the modal theory. The formula ($A_a p \ \& \ \sim A_a p$) is contradictory only under the interpretation *de dicto (in sensu composito)*, not under the interpretation *de re (in sensu diviso)*. But to have an interpretation *de re* one has to think, as I stated

---

[10] On the problems of 'beginning' and 'ending' see John Murdoch, »Infinity and continuity», *LMP* p. 285—287.

above, that there is a different temporal point for having an assent and not having it. It is typical for St. Thomas, however, that he did not quite realize the implications of this modal distinction because of his modal and teleological presuppositions.[11] That is the reason why opinion does not clearly identify itself with an act, attitude or habit, but is characterized by them all.

It would be more convenient to propose for (D) the following implication

$$(D_{impl}) \qquad D_a p \supset \sim A_a p \& \sim A_a \sim p.$$

If we take this as a characterization of doubt then it is clear that the consequent part of the implication could mean a mere absence of any assent from which it does not follow that doubt is an act. Therefore, St. Thomas could try and save himself from inconsistency by saying that a person opines inconsistently only if he actively and in full awareness refrains from assenting i.e. performs an act of doubting, but that he is not inconsistent if he opines by assenting merely with the possibility of the contradictory being true without actively thinking it. Putting an act and a mere privation on a par may have had an influence on St. Thomas' inconsistent formulation and on the built-in asymmetry between doubting and not-doubting so that the implication $D_a p \supset D_a \sim p$ is not always valid. In this sense there is some conceptual or intensional looseness in (D).

8.4 Different assents in epistemic contexts

In characterizing the notions of ordinary belief and knowledge St. Thomas also makes good use of assent, and what is more, in a precisely similar way. We first get the description

$$(K_T) \qquad K_a p = A_a p \& \sim A_a \sim p$$

for knowledge and the description

$$(B_T) \qquad B_a p = A_a p \& \sim A_a \sim p$$

---

[11] See Simo Knuuttila, »Time and Modality in Scholasticism», *Reforging the Great Chain of Being*. Studies of the History of Modal Theories. Ed. S. Knuuttila, Synthese Historical Library 20, Dordrecht-Holland/Boston-U.S.A./London-England, p. 163—257.

for ordinary belief. Amazingly, the descriptions are similar, but when we consider the notions in question more closely it will become apparent that they are not equivalent.

Opinion, ordinary belief, faith and (scientific) knowledge are all different matters for St. Thomas, although he fluctuates somewhat between the points of view to be taken. In any case he emphasizes that a man can become exercised in his assenting either to a contingent or to a necessary object.[12] Therefore, the very assent as an act is the same, only its objects are different, respectively the attitudes as habits are different, too.[13] If scientific knowledge and ordinary belief are similar only for the part of assent as an act it may tell us that the will has an important role for both. We shall turn to this in a moment.

If there were no other difference between knowledge and ordinary belief than the existence of different objects then (B_T) and (K_T) would only suggest that as soon as a person assents consistently he knows or believes. This sounds very trivial. We will grasp a very interesting difference, however, if we notice that the interpretation of assent is not quite the same in the characterizations of St. Thomas. He namely says that assent in (K_T) is »caused», but is not in (B_T).[14]

The assent which is born from the »causation of cogitation» may lead to two kinds of knowledge: it may be the knowledge which consists of the assent to a self-evident proposition: this is understanding *(intellectus)*. But it may also be knowledge which is born from rational argumentation: this is scientific knowledge *(scientia)*. In both cases the assent which is born has been caused by something which can »move» the intellect: either by a self-evident or an analytical manner *(notis terminis)*

---

[12] Originally St. Thomas seems to think that the faculties in question are different on the basis of different objects suggesting that he has an Aristotelean basis for this, rather than a Platonic one. See *De ver.* 15, 2 ad 3; 2 ad 12 and ad 14; E. F. Byrne, *Probabilty and Opinion.* A Study in the Medieval Presuppositions of Post-Medieval theories of Probability. The Hague 1968, p. 73. Later, however, St. Thomas seems to reject the view that science and opinion would be different faculties on the basis of objects alone, because the same faculty can have a necessary as well as a contingent object. See *PP* 79, 9 ad 3; Byrne (1968) p. 74.

[13] In all this St. Thomas thinks to do justice to Aristotle, but it is clear that his standpoint is a compromise between Plato and Aristotle. See Byrne (1968) p. 74—75, especially footnote 1, p. 75.

[14] *De ver.* 14, 1: »Sciens vero habet . . . cogitationem causantem assensum et assensum terminantem cogitationem.»

or in a mediate way by rational reasons *(virtute principiorum).*[15] In one passage St. Thomas expresses this as follows:

> Now there are two ways in which the intellect assents to anything. One way is by being actuated by the object to which it assents: the intellect may know this object immediately, as in the case of first principles, the object of understanding, or it may know it mediately, as in the case of conclusions, the object of science.[16]

What is important to notice here is that the condition of justification, being absent from the characterization of knowledge in (K_T), is slipped in through the back door disguised as a specific assent.

In the case of belief the assent is different. In spite of having a similar characterization, belief is distinguished from knowledge by not having any conclusive reasons or causes which would bring about the assent.[17] Assenting is now performed by choice either with weak or full certainty. In the latter case the certainty is conceived as not dependent on the rational epistemic factors at all; on the contrary, assenting is based on the will, as St. Thomas says:

> The other way the intellect assents is not through a sufficient motivation by its proper object, but through some voluntary choice that influences the intellect in favour of one alternative rather than the other. And if this happens with doubt and with fear that the contradictory might not be true, it is opinion; if, however, it happens with certainty and without any such fear, it is faith.[18]

We see that opinion and ordinary belief differ from each other in the way expressed by (O) and (B_T), but also through the interpretation of assent as change, and finally that opinion and faith differ from each other

---

[15] See *De ver.* 14, 1.

[16] *SS,* 1, 4: »Assentit autem intellectus alicui dupliciter. Uno modo, quia ad hoc movetur ab ipso objecto quod est per seipsum cognitum, sicut patet in principiis primis, quorum est intellectus, vel est per aliud cognitum, sicut patet de conclusionibus, quarum est scientia.»

[17] As a truthful pupil of Aristotle St. Thomas says in this connection that beliefs are similar to axioms in the sense that they are certain, but not proved. See *Comm. in Anal. post.* I, 44, n. 399: ». . . acceptio idest existimatio quaedam, immediatae propositionis et non necessariae».

[18] *Ibid.* »Alio modo, intellectus assentit alicui non quia sufficienter moveatur ab objecto proprio, sed per quandam electionem voluntarie declinans in unam partem magis quam in aliam. Et si quidem haec sit cum dubitatione et formidine alterius partis, erit opinio; si autem sit cum certitudine absque tali formidine, erit fides.»

through the grade of certainty, faith being a relatively independent attitude. But it is interesting that no attention is payed to the difference between ordinary belief and faith in the characterization above. What is the difference between (B$_T$) and faith? The answer is partly that *'credere'* (believe) is used by St. Thomas as a wider classificatory term; opinion and faith tend to be its species. But there are also deeper reasons for complexity here.

As we saw (K$_T$) has essentially the trait of the terminating of cogitation; likewise, it is as essential to (B$_T$) that cogitation does not terminate. Why is this so? The answer seems to be that in the case of knowledge St. Thomas accpets the condition of truth, in the case of ordinary belief he rejects it. Thinking will end in the former case, because in knowing the intellect has reached its object i.e. truth and cannot go any further. Instead, in the latter case, when somebody believes that p, the intellect can always go further, because it has not reached conclusive grounds for seeing the truth.[19] St. Thomas takes this to mean that whereas in the former case the object to be reached itself causes the act of knowing (*»movetur ab ipso objecto«*), in the latter case there must be some other factor for causing the act. This is the will. Therefore, the relationship between cogitation and will is a supplementary one in the case of belief.[20]

There also seems to be another idea very closely linked to the different handling of the condition of truth. By knowing (scientifically or ideally) that p, the intellect has reached such a proposition that its truth value cannot change, for p is eternal, necessary and immutable. The propositions which are the objects of belief are contingent and mutable; their truth value can change. Therefore, the act of the intellect is in the former case *once and for all;* in the latter case there must be *repeated acts*

---

[19] *SS* 2, 1: »Sed actus iste qui est credere habet firmam adhaesionem ad unam partem, in quo convenit credens cum sciente et intelligente; et tamen ejus cognitio non est perfecta per manifestam visionem, in quo convenit cum dubitante, suspicante et opinante.«

[20] *De ver.* 14. 1: »Quandoque vero intellectus non potest determinari ad alteram partem contradictionis neque statim per ipsas definitiones terminorum, sicut in principiis, nec etiam virtute principiorum, sicut est in conclusionibus demonstrationis; determinatur autem per voluntatem, quae eligit assentire uni parti determinate praecise propter aliquid, quod est sufficiens ad movendum voluntatem, non autem ad movendum intellectum, utpote quia videtur bonum vel conveniens huic parti assentire, et ista est dispositio credentis, ut cum aliquis credit dictis alicuius hominis, quia videtur ei decens vel utile.«

of the intellect caused by the will, because there is no connection of the intellect with any such object which would cause the act.

So far it is clear that we need reformulations of (K_T) and (B_T). We have to express the different assents involved in the formulations. Thus, for knowledge we need

$$(K_T') \qquad K_a p \; =^{\text{cog.caus.}} \; A_a p \; \& \; \sim A_a \sim p$$

and for belief

$$(B_T') \qquad B_a p \; =^{\text{vol.caus.}} \; A_a p \; \& \; \sim A_a \sim p.$$

The assent of knowledge can be called *informative* or *causative* and the assent of belief *decisional* or *volitive*. The former has an Aristotelean origin, the latter an Augustinian. The main result, however, is that ordinary belief and knowledge are continuous, receiving mutually exclusive limit values: cogitation and volition; termination of cogitation and non-volition in knowledge, non-termination of cogitation and volition in ordinary belief. Our next question, then, will be: How far, if at all, is faith in the same continuum?

8.5 Belief and faith

I said earlier that faith may be considered as a species of belief. This, however, is qualified in many ways. Opinion was differentiated from ordinary belief by the property of being a kind of internal change, which means that opinions as such can be taken as parameters.[21] Ordinary beliefs, in a sense, can be considered as borderline cases of opinions, because they have a firm object *whenever* they have it. But it does not follow that a person by an ordinary belief always blieves what he once believes. At another time he could believe otherwise. Faith seems to have some traits similar to belief, some dissimilar.[22]

The objects of faith cannot change: firstly, in the sense that they cannot as propositions change from true to false, and secondly in the sense

---

[21] Opinions in this sense can be taken as having, on the whole, different values between 0—1, which implies a kind of symmetry of $D_a p$ and D_a-p, namely, that (intensionally) the former having a value e.g. 0.45 equals to the latter having the value 0.55, which are not values of p and -p. See Byrne (1968) p. 265—267.

[22] Because St. Thomas uses the verb *credere* for faith it is not always easy to say what differences of meaning are implied. Cf. *SS* 2, 2.

that they are immutable *enuntiabilia*.[23] In the first sense they are immutable and contingent truths, in the second sense they are ontologically specific entities. Obviously, the status implied by the latter was seen by St. Thomas as necessary to protect the view in the former.

But faith is similar to belief in that it presupposes repeated acts for the purpose of creating a standing state, habitus. It might seem somewhat peculiar that St. Thomas assigns a perpetual cogitation both to ordinary belief and to faith, although faith seems to imply the acceptance of the condition of truth and thereby the termination of cogitation. An explanation might be offered that he wants to conserve the Augustinian programme of *fides quaerens intellectum*. We shall see that the implicit and explicit teleology are, in the last analysis, better candidates to explain St. Thomas' epistemic ideas.

The most striking dissimilarities between faith and belief are two in number: faith is absolutely certain and it has peculiar objects, namely, revelatory propositions. But then the question is: Is faith able to remain within the realm of belief any more?

8.6 The enigmatic status of revelatory propositions

According to St. Thomas the set of revelatory propositions differs from the set of natural propositions because the former set is not knowable by the natural reason. One of the reasons for this is that the revelatory propositions cannot inform the intellect by transferring a *form* into the intellect. The ability or inability of information is expressed by St. Thomas usually with the help of the distinction *visum — non-visum*. The propositions of faith are not seen, and therefore they are not informed either.[24]

In order to understand what this all is about, we have to remember that »complex» and »non-complex» understanding are different. The latter always has as its object some thing *(res)*, the former some proposition. The latter is called *apprehensio simplex,* the former *apprehensio*

---

[23] The objects of faith are only true propositions. See *SS* 1, 3: »Unde nihil potest cadere sub fide nisi inquantum stat sub veritate prima. Sub qua nullum falsum stare potest . . . Unde relinquitur quod fidei non potest subesse aliquod falsum.» St. Thomas also accepts a similar view of the semantics of the objects of faith to that of St. Bonaventura. See *Quodlibeta* 4, 17; *In Sent.,* Dist. 41, 1, 5; *PP* 14, 15.

[24] See e.g. *SS* 171, 2; *SS* 1, 4; *De ver.* 14, 1 ad 5.

complexa. The cause of a revelatory proposition is a *res,* namely God which is The Primary Cause. But the human mind cannot receive any immediate form from God, nor can it scientifically know the primary causation. Consequently, God as being *(res)* cannot be the object of the non-complex understanding.[25]

Nevertheless, the complex understanding can be composed of propositions of God. These propositions are not born in the usual scientific way, namely, by the abstraction of the so-called »substantial forms» (essences) from created beings. In this sense we cannot know anything of God, because the substantial forms of created beings as well as metaphysical categories are not properties of God.[26] Therefore, God must reveal in a specific way the propositions that concern himself.

In addition, in these revealed propositions certain weak forms of supernatural realities are transmitted to the intellect; typically St. Thomas uses the term *impressio* in this connection.[27] From the point of view of scientific knowledge revealed propositions are imperfect; therefore, their power of information is insufficient: they are anticipations *(praelibationes)* and enigmas *(aenigmae).*[28] But because they are able to transmit »a similitude of the uncreated truth» caused by *gratia infusa,* they are, semantically speaking, *enuntiabilia,* which can be *analogically* applied to God.[29]

---

[25] According to St. Thomas it is impossible to have an »apprehensio simplex» of The First Truth. See *PP* 85, 5; *SS* 1, 1—2; *PP* 16, 1—2, 5.

[26] There is a serious problem concerning the totality of forms in God, because as St. Thomas says, ideas or forms cannot be outside God. But then they seem to become God's own attributes. See H. A. Wolfson, *Religious Philosophy: A Group of Essays.* Atheneum — New York 1965, p. 60—62.

[27] »Impressio veritatis primae», *PP* 88, 3 ad 1; »sigillatio quedam primae veritatis in mente», *De Trin.* 1, 1, 1—4. St. Thomas mostly uses the Anselmian locution 'veritas prima' and the Augustinian, according to which The First Truth prints a concept into mind »as an impression of The Good itself». See *De ver.* 14, 1 ad 7; *SS* 4, 1; St. Augustine, *De Trin.* VIII, 3, 4.

[28] It is to be remembered that the supreme end is cognitive, therefore 'praelibatio' and 'aenigma' are used in a cognitive context here. See *SS* 2, 3—4; *PP* 13, 3; *De ver.* 14, 2 ad 9 and ad 15: »quedam praelibatio brevis totius operis sequentis» (scientific argumentation), »ipsa fides est quedam praelibatio brevis cognitionis quam in futuro habebimus» (faith).

[29] ». . . similitudo increatae veritatis in nobis», *De ver.* 11, 1; cf. *PP* 88, 3 and *PS* 109, 1. According to St. Thomas there is a linguistic name for each article of faith and a meaning, *enuntiabile,* corresponding each name. *PP* 14, 15.

8.7 Twofold »motion»

St. Thomas' teleological presuppositions implied that man's directness to the Supreme End, Primary Truth and Good, is reflected in his cognitive attitudes. As I have already stated this directness involves cognitive motion: to become informed or advanced in achieving the forms of the created world.[30] But how, in the case of faith, is this motion to be understood? It is here where St. Thomas' Augustinism and Aristoteleanism create their greatest tension.

St. Thomas speaks of the »initiative» *(inchoatio)* of possessing the Supreme Good and Truth already in this life.[31] The final end, the beatific vision of God, cannot be achieved on this life, but it can get started already here. Epistemologically this means that a certain dynamic cognitive privation remains to be completed in the future life. What about the role of faith in these dynamics?

Interestingly enough, St. Thomas has a somewhat obscure answer to this question. He seems to be trying to say something like the following: In the metaphysical process of perfection faith will be completed by its changing into vision when faith is considered from the point of view of the *form*. But if faith is considered from the viewpoint of its *end* it will be completed by producing in man a habit whereby his will is constantly directed to the Supreme Good. How is this to be understood?[32]

I shall propose the following hypothesis: *the cognitive acquisition of information and the motion caused by will are entangled in each other.* Being touched by the essences (substantial forms) of things generally de-

---

[30] See *SS* 171, 2: »Principium autem eorum quae ad supernaturalem cognitionem pertinent . . . est ipse Deus»; *PS* 109, 1: »Non solum autem a Deo est omnis motio sicut a primo movente; sed etiam ab ipso est omnis formalis perfectio sicut a primo actu.» Cf. *PS* 106, 1 ad 2; *PP* 79, 4—5; *PS* 62, 4; *PP* 12, 7; 84, 3; *PP* 16. 3.

[31] See *De ver.* 14, 2: ». . . nihil autem potest ordinari in aliquem finem nisi praeexistat in ipso quedam proportio ad finem, ex qua proveniat in ipso desiderium finis; et hoc est secundum quod aliqua finis inchoatio fit in ipso,»Cf. *PP* 1, 4.

[32] See *SS* 2, 3: ». . . ultima beatitudo hominis consistit in quadam supernaturali Dei visione.» This end is at the same time the *form* of the object of faith. See *De ver.* 14, 2 ad 10: ». . . actus fidei essentialiter consistit in cognitione, et ibi est eius perfectio quantum ad formam vel speciem, . . ., sed quantum ad finem perficitur in affectione,» cf. *ibid.:* ». . . fides est habitus mentis, qua inchoatur vita aeterna in nobis faciens intellectum non apparentibus assentire,» See also: *SS* 4, 1; *PS* 51, 4.

fines the ends to be achieved by practical action. This is an Aristotelean as well as a Platonic conception. The main idea of so-called *prohairesis* is that if we have knowledge of the form then we automatically know what to do and set out to do it. In the case of St. Thomas, because faith is directed to God and it is cognitively imperfect, it does not achieve its object directly. Earlier I said that faith seems to imply the acceptance of the condition of truth. Now, this has to be a very peculiar kind of acceptance. Namely, in the pure cognitive sense the object of faith cannot be present, in this life, but *implicitly* it may be present. The content of faith consists of anticipated supernatural forms of the Supreme Truth. These forms can be actualized only by the implicit habit of faith i.e. the forms are seen to be achieved by this habit. Therefore, these forms are not cognitively present, but only present *in virtue*. In addition, because there cannot be any falsehood or failure in having faith, there is, in a sense, an acceptance of the condition of truth: what is believed by faith must be true, if not seen to be true objectively, although, being true of the believer as his real property. Because this is not a purely cognitive acceptance of the condition of truth, it can best be understood as an instance of implicit teleology. But how is this claim to be explained?

We can get support for our hypothesis, for example, from the passage where St. Thomas reports of prophetic knowledge. For supernatural knowledge we need, he firstly says, light which exceeds the natural light of reason. Then he continues:

> But light can inhere in something in two ways: firstly, by a permanent form as the material light is in sun and in fire; secondly, by a way of some penetrating *property* or *impression* as the light is in the air.[33]

This is, of course, a metaphoric expression: however, something can be derived from it. We know that the term *'passio'* was normally used in scholastic discussions to stand for an attribute or property. Therefore, it is quite clear that St. Thomas wants to say here that faith as well as light is, at the same time, a penetrating property of man's life as well as an impression of a form. This simply means that supernatural forms are not properly forms in the intellect, but forms which give form to one's

---

[33] See *SS* 171, 2: »Lumen autem dupliciter alicui inesse potest: uno modo, per modum formae permanentis, sicut lumen corporale est in sole et in igne; alio modo, per modum cuiusdam *passionis* sive *impressionis* traseuntis, sicut lumen est in aere.» Cf. *PP* 69, 1 ad 1.

life i.e. forms which define the ends and efforts of man. Nevertheless, again we see how the teleological way of thinking is revealed not only explicitly, but implicitly, too. The presence of a divine form as a quality of life tends to imply the presence of the objects of faith, not only cognitively, but existing as the habitual qualities in the soul. As a habit faith has an enigmatically actualized form in the present state, but this form cannot be a pure potentiality because in that case it would not become actualised until in future. Because the form is *somehow* actualized already in the present state it is *between* the actual and the potential.[34] Therefore, faith is not knowledge explicitly satisfying the condition of truth, but quasi-knowledge implicitly satisfying the condition of truth.

Another support for our hypothesis is receivable from the difficult and many-sided discussion concerning the theory of agent and possible intellect. St. Thomas rejects the Augustinian theory of illumination, the theory of the plurality of substantial forms in man, and the theory of the active and potential intellect as separate entities; the last mentioned are only »powers of the soul» *(potentiae animae).*[35] These rejections, however, do not prevent him from making an important distinction between the first and second »intentions».[36] The status of second intentions is not unambiguous, because in a certain sense they are second order concepts concerning the first order concepts. Therefore, in a very literal sense, what the second intentions purport to be is seeing the reality in the »light» of concepts which organize or bear upon the first order concepts. St. Thomas admits that there are such second order concepts which are on a par with metaphysical categories. To this extent he is an Augustinian. But he denies that these concepts have any ontological status of their own; on the contrary, they are attributes of the soul without any independent existence.[37]

---

[34] Cf. *SS* 171, 2: »Habitus autem est forma permanens,» *PP* 87, 2: »Habitus quodammodo est medium inter potentiam et purum actum,» cf. *SS* 4, 1; *De ver.* 14, 2; *PP* 109, 1; *PS* 62, 3; *SS* 4, 1. Notice that motions are labelled by the term at the end (ad quem), see *PS* 113, 1. Notice also that similitude holds between the end and the form of man's life, see *De ver.* 11, 1 ad 3; Kenny (1980) p. 72.

[35] See *De anima* 3; *De unitate intellectus contra Averroistas* chapters 1, 4—5; Weisheipl (1974) p. 252—253, 276—279.

[36] See *PS* 109, 1; *PS* 62, 3; Robert W. Schmidt, *The Domain of Logic according to St. Thomas Aquinas.* Martinus Niihoff, The Hague 1966, p. 311—319; Byrne (1968) p. 259, 263; compare *PP* 84, 3; 84, 8.

[37] See *PP* 84, 5; 85, 1.

The most essential conclusion to be drawn here, especially from the point of view of St. Thomas' Aristoteleanism, is that although we can speak of »divine illuminaton» we have to concede (with Aristotle) that second order ideas which relate everything to God do not have a standard epistemological status; they do not properly belong to the circle of theoretical knowledge, rather they belong to the circle of practical knowledge. But because St. Thomas does not make very clear statements here, the status of these second intentions or ideas fluctuates; they are very naturally interpreted as implicit tendencies towards God reflected both cognitively as »light», and virtually as »moved» by action.

So far we have seen, I hope, that without our explanation on the basis of implicit teleology it would be quite incomprehensible how the cognitive realisation of a supernatural form and practical action could be united. Conceptually separated notions would remain. It follows that scholars who have offered an explanation by speaking of the »light of faith» in terms of purely cognitive categories do not do justice to St. Thomas. But why could it not be that St. Thomas simply accepts an explicit teleology in this connection? This question requires a further scrutiny of Timothy Potts' views.

8.8 Potts' analysis

In his article »Aquinas on Belief and Faith» Timothy Potts presents the following thesis concerning St. Thomas' view of believing:

(T$_P$) $B_a p$ if and only if a accepts that p because he wishes that q, where accepting that p is a necessary means to q.[38]

In the same context Potts asks whether the condition »accepting that p is a necessary means to q» is a kind of *meta-belief, meta-knowledge* or *meta-opinion*. This question can also be applied to faith, says Potts. Then we will have a reformulation of (T$_P$) as follows:

(F$_P$) $B_a p$ by faith if and only if a accepts that p as a revelatory proposition because he wishes that q, which implies the vision of God, where accepting that p is a necessary means to q.[39]

---

[38] See Potts (1971) p. 8.
[39] See Potts (1971) p. 19.

But what do we mean by 'meta-belief' here? There are at least two interpretations readily at hand: (1) one believes that in some situation a's accepting that p is a necessary means to q, or (2) one believes that q in itself entails the willing of a means. These are two quite different meta-beliefs. If Potts is trying to build his theory on the first interpretation, then the implicit teleology will be overlooked. We have to try and clarify these problematic formulations.[40]

The explanatory idea in Potts' thesis seems to be the notion of *efficient willing (voluntas efficialis)*. According to Potts' thesis St. Thomas' thought follows the scheme of the so-called practical syllogism which can be formulated e.g. by saying that the first premiss expresses a state of affairs as an object of willing and the second premiss expresses a belief which is considered as a necessary means to achieving this state of affairs. Let us suppose that 'q' stands for a state of affairs, say that of the vision of God, 'W' is the intensional operator for willing and '$B_a p$' stands for a belief of a revelatory proposition, say that God is triune. Now we could formulate the practical syllogism in question as follows:

(i) $W_a q$

(ii) $\sim B_a p \supset \sim q$

(iii) $B_a p$

If between q and $B_a p$ a consequential relationship holds then the following inference, with certain reservations,[41] should be valid:

$$\frac{\vdash q \supset B_a p}{W_a q \supset W_a B_a p}$$

From this in turn we could with the help of contraposition infer:

$$\frac{W_a q \supset W_a B_a p}{\sim W_a B_a p \supset \sim W_a q}$$

---

[40] Potts' formulation is not unambiguous because there is nothing which would clearly state whether 'accepting that p is a necessary means to q' *is one of a's own beliefs*.

[41] The step from the formula $\sim B_a p \supset \sim q$ to the formula $q \supset B_a p$ presupposes the validity of contraposition in this connection. The validity can be disputed, but it can also be defended by conceiving for it a domain of all those possible worlds where the end q can be realized only with the help of relevant means. The other inference above is perhaps also restricted because it presupposes among other things that a fully understands what follows logically from q.

The last inference says that if somebody does not want to believe that God is triune then he, *eo ipso,* does not want to see God. The idea of efficient willing is simply that *willing the end implies willing the means.* This, however, as such does not confirm the influence of the implicit teleology in St. Thomas' thought; we should still show that the connection between the end and believing in premiss (ii) is somewhat logical or conceptual i.e. $\vdash q \supset B_a p$.

Somebody could perhaps tell us as *argumentum ex silentio* that nowhere does St. Thomas say that the meta-belief would imply the above-mentioned conceptual implication. I would like to answer, first, that the basic conceptual presuppositions are almost never explicitly formulated by the thinkers. In addition, there seem to be some sayings of St. Thomas which support my claim. Let us consider that the meta-belief in question were formulated.

$$(11) \qquad B_a(q \supset B_a p).$$

Now, this can be understood that if somebody believes that realizing an end implies believing in a certain means then this person *in his own mind does not think there could be a counterexample of this.* I.e. this person could not say in the first person singular: I believe that my believing is a means to an end, but it is not so. In this case the implication here is, even if not an ordinary logical one, an *intensional* or *conceptual* one. St. Thomas gives some support to our view by saying e.g. that »the willed is somehow present in the willer» and »the willed is not only the goal, but also what leads to this goal».[42] What is more, he says that as soon something appears »decent and useful» to the will this something is able to move the will.[43] According to St. Thomas it is impossible to think that when something is an end to someone this person would not simul-

---

[42] See *PS* 16, 4: »Respondeo dicendum quod voluntas duplicem habitudinem habet ad volitum. Unam quidem, secundum quod volitum est quodammodo in volente, per quandam proportionem vel ordinem ad volitum. . . . Volitum autem non solum est finis, sed id quod est ad finem.»

[43] See *De ver.* 14, 1: ». . . propter aliquid, quod est sufficiens ad movendum voluntatem, . . . , utpote quia videtur bonum vel conveniens huic parti assentire. Et ista est dispositio credentis, ut cum aliquis credit dictis alicuius hominis, quia videtur ei decens vel utile, et sic etiam movemur ad credendum dictis dei, inquantum nobis repromittitur, si crediderimus, praemium aeternae vitae: et hoc praemio moventur voluntas . . .»

taneously will the means to this end. This is a very strong teleological postulate because according to it there could not be no end without it being pursued. If this is so then it is clear that St. Thomas' standpoint includes some kind of a conceptual tie between an end and willing the means to this end. Because the end and the means cannot be *thought* of independently, it is, again, an instance of implicit teleology.

We supposed earlier that from the formula $W_aq \supset W_aB_ap$ we can take an inference step to the formula $\sim W_aB_ap \supset \sim W_aq$ which, as I said, would presuppose the acceptance of the contraposition principle in this connection. It would follow, accordingly, that it would be somehow logically or conceptually erroneous to will that q without willing to believe that p. That St. Thomas, in fact, thinks in this way is verified to some extent starting from his saying (which refers to St. Augustine): »without willing man can do some other things, but not believing».[44] This thought could be expressed in a strong form by the formula

$$(12) \qquad \sim B_ap \supset \sim W_aB_ap.$$

If now also the contraposition formula of the above

$$(13) \qquad \sim W_aB_ap \supset \sim W_aq$$

were valid then we would have

$$(14) \qquad \sim B_ap \supset \sim W_aq.$$

We might accept (13) here because it says that if somebody is not willing to believe anything (as a means) he is not willing any end whatsoever. Then we would have a consequence (14) i.e. that if somebody does not believe anything he is not willing any end either, in other words, if he wills something, he believes something, too. This, as such, is very problematic seen from our point of view, because wanting an end needs not logically force us to believe anything at all.[45]

From the point of view of St. Thomas the situation is different. Because (14) does not appear explicitly formulated, even though it is a suit-

---

[44] See *De ver.* 14, 1: ». . . et ideo dicit augustinus quod cetera potest homo nolens, credere non nisi volens»; cf. St. Augustine, *De spiritu et littera* 31, 54.

[45] There are many logical obscurities here, e.g., if we would take (12) as a valid theorem in the combined logic of belief and will, it would not be clear whether everybody always believes what he wants, or that if somebody believes something he also wants to believe it.

able formulation for expressing implicit teleology in this context, but appears only as a consequence from (12) and (13), then there is a tendency of implicit teleology at work here, provided that St. Thomas accepted (12) and (13). The former he accepted, as I mentioned, in terms of St. Augustine, the latter e.g. by saying that eternal reward (end) moves our will to believe (as means) the words of God.[46] Therefore, what was Potts' concern points to an implicit meta-belief. That means that our main conclusion is: according to St. Thomas it is somehow *conceptually erroneous* to want something without combining it with belief.

There is one additional point to be made. The teleological explanation fits very well the syllogistic inference scheme which was the basic form for all logical thinking in St. Thomas as well as in other scholastics. Therefore, what is needed is only to put willing into the place of the middle term:

(1)   eternal reward → willing
(2)   willing → believing
---
(3)   eternal reward → believing[47]

Because willing, in a way, transmits the form included in the eternal reward, namely, the form which is not achievable by purely cognitive means, then we are precisely on the syllogistic road starting from the end, q, and arriving at the means, believing. But having the *status* of a middle term in a syllogism, willing represents a conceptual link rather than a factual one, because it is something which not only practically, but also logically combines a premiss and a consequence i.e. terms denoting the end and the means. Therefore, this point also supports the explanation on the basis of implicit teleology.

8.9 The condition of truth

So far I have tried to give some evidence that in a way, namely by the metaphysical and conceptual implications of motion, faith satisfies the condition of truth. This means that faith and science have a similarity of being unable to fail in achieving the truth i.e. the formulas

---

[46] See footnote 20.
[47] See *De ver.* 14, 1, footnote 20 above.

(1) $K_a p \supset p$

and

(1') $B^{faith}_a p \supset p$

would seem to be adopted by St. Thomas. However, according to him there are some important restrictions in interpreting these conditions. For us it is important to take into account these restrictions because they are, as it were, milestones in the history of epistemic and doxastic logic. For example, if one accepts (1) and (1') and in addition the condition of consistency for one's propositional attitude it would follow that one has adopted an epistemically relevant concept of religious faith; no independent »logic of faith» or autonomous »religious language» whatsoever would exist. Because we know that history brought up these kinds of ideas already in Late Scholasticism, it is important to have as clear a view as possible of the position of St. Thomas in this development.

The first interesting restriction concerns (1). St. Thomas seems to think that although in the case of scientific knowledge (1) has to be valid, it is restricted by the demand of omnitemporality: what we scientifically know has to be true always. Therefore, if we know something now and this something no longer holds tomorrow St. Thomas would say that we would no longer know it tomorrow.[48] This would mean a temporal restriction for (1), namely

(1^t) $K_a p_{to} \supset p_{to}$

from which it would naturally follow

(15) $\sim p_{to} \supset \sim K_a p_{to}$

which states that whenever something is not the case it could not be known, which sounds absurd to the modern ears because we claim to know e.g. past events. For St. Thomas it was not so absurd because he thought in the Aristotelean manner that knowledge in the proper scientific sense has to be linked with something which is always. So, (1^t) does not apply to proper knowledge, unless under the interpretation of omnitemporality. Temporally changing truths are not objects of proper knowledge, but of *opinion*.[49]

---

[48] In this St. Thomas is in concordance with Aristotle see *Cateqories* 7, 7b; St. Thomas, *In metaphysicam* VII, lectio 15, 1610—1612; cf. *PS* 10, 2 ad 2.

[49] See *PS* 10, 2 ad 3; Byrne (1968) p. 178—179.

St. Thomas' discussion is illuminating on the two ways by which we can fail to keep knowledge in the soul. We can fail through the intellectual act changing or by the object changing.[50] There can be two relevant intellectual acts: simple apprehension and predicative apprehension. In the former case there is no possibility of failing, in the latter there is.[51] The idea implied in the former case seems to be Anselmian

(7') $Tp/x \supset p/x$

where 'x' is a variable for substantial form. But this would mean that the condition of truth were restricted to some cases of knowledge by *acquaintance* e.g. 'knowing who' or 'knowing what'. Furthermore, the predicative intellectual act can be false in two ways: if one changes his attitude and the object prevails, and if one does not change one's attitude and the object changes. This shows that St. Thomas was relying on the presupposition of the so-called statistical modal theory in understanding the metalogical criterion of truth.[52] If the person has something *immutable all the time* as the object of his intellect the condition of truth is most likely to be applicable. Model candidates for this case are intellectual *acquaintances*.

What about the condition of truth in connection with faith? We have already seen some qualifications and restrictions in its application. As a habit, faith is something »becoming» or »actualizing» all the time, as I have stated earlier. I have also hinted at St. Thomas' locution according to which »fidei non potest subesse aliquod falsum». These two ideas must be combined. The interesting point, then, is that although the

---

[50] See *PP* 16, 8: »Quae quidem conformitas variari potest dupliciter, sicut et quaelibet alia similitudo, ex mutatione alterius extremi. Unde uno modo variatur veritas ex parte intellectus, ex eo quod de re eodem modo se habente aliquis aliam opinionem accipit: alio modo si, opinione eadem manente, res mutetur. Et utroque modo fit mutatio de vero in falsum.»

[51] *PP* 85, 6: »Obiectum autem proprium intellectus est quidditas rei. Unde circa quidditatem rei, per se loquendo, intellectus non fallitur. Sed circa ea quae circumstant rei essentiam vel quidditatem, intellectus potest falli.»

[52] See *PP* 16, 8 ad 3: »Sic igitur haec propositio, *Socrates sedet,* eo sedente vera est et veritate rei, inquantum est quedam vox significativa; et veritate significationis, inquantum significat opinionem veram. Socrate vero surgente, remanet prima veritas, sed mutatur secunda.» Cf. Aristotle's Modal Theory *Metaph.* 1047a 12—14; 1047b 4—6; *De Interpret.* 19a 23—24; Knuuttila, »Time and Modality in Scholasticism» (1981) p. 163—257.

intellect may possess some kinds of forms, namely *»praelibationes»*, these are not infallible objects of simple apprehension. However, they are always true. Therefore, (1') cannot be unqualifiably valid. It is valid only in the sense that a person *continuously exercises his intellect not to change* the acts which have revealed supernatural truths as their objects. By continuously assenting to these propositions, faith becomes a habit. This means that the metalogical condition of truth is accepted by St. Thomas in the sense where it depends on whether faith has become a habit or not. Because the objects of faith never change, wrong faith is only produced by a wrong act. Therefore, the acceptance of the condition of truth is possible only on the restriction that one never makes a vicious, i.e. an unorthodox, act or faith. From the modern point of view we could say that the condition of truth for faith is according to St. Thomas valid only for the world where, by continuous assenting, the objects of faith are always kept in sight.

8.10 Certainty

In speaking of certainty St. Thomas makes two distinctions: *absolute — probable* and *causal — proof*. The first distinction is very obscure. What St. Thomas probably wants to say is that the notion of certainty is analysable in principle from two different aspects: by considering certainty as a parameter or by considering it as a constant. As a parameter certainty may have a variable value between 0 and 1 and it can be understood mentally (subjectively) or ontologically (objectively). As a constant certainty may also be understood both mentally and ontologically, but its role is that of an intensional operator, not that of a variable. However, in some places St. Thomas seems to think that certainty as a constant could be understood as a limit value of a parameter. Under that interpretation the limit value of a mental opinion is mental certainty and the limit case of an ontological contingency is an ontological certainty (or necessity).[53]

---

[53] There is also a distinction *essentialiter — participative* which multiplies the complexity of St. Thomas' thought. See *SS* 18, 4: »Certitudo invenitur in aliquo dupliciter: scilicet essentialiter, et participative. Essentialiter quidem invenitur in vi cognoscitiva: participative autem in omni eo quod a vi cognoscitiva movetur infallibiliter ad finem suum.» the notion of probability is also involved here. Probable cer-

The second distinction is more transparent. There are matters which are certain on the basis of their certain cause, and matters which are certain on the basis of the proof which can be given. Because man does not always see the certainty of cause, he may have certainty of cause without certainty of proof. In these cases man automatically reaches the truth. But it follows paradoxically that man can simultaneously be less certain of matters of which he otherwise is absolutely certain. This is because of the non-identity of these two certainties. This is precisely the situation in the case of the certainty of faith and scientific knowledge. The difference is that the absolute and ontological certainty of cause can occur simultaneously with the weak cognitive status of proof; therefore, the mental status can differ from that of the cause. This is expressed by St. Thomas as follows:

> As to the intellectual virtues: certitude has two aspects. The one depends on its cause: whatever has a more certain cause is itself more certain. In this respect faith has greater certitude than the other three, for faith is grounded on divine truth; the other three, on human reasoning. The other aspect of certitude depends on its possessor: for anyone what is more certain is what his mind penetrates more fully. By this measure faith is less certain, since the things of faith surpass the human mind, whereas the objects of intellectual virtues do not.[54]

Here we see that St. Thomas accepted two notions of certainty so that the formula

(16) $V_a p \ \& \ \sim V'_a p$

should be valid. But what are the implications of these two notions for faith?

---

tainty reaches the truth »ut in pluribus», absolute certainty is expressed by nature's infallible causes (causae determinatae) »ut semper». See *In IV liber. sent.* I, 38, 1, 5c; *SS* 70, 2; *In I liber. ethic.* 3b: »Non enim potest esse tanta certitudo in materia variabili, et contingenti, sicut in materia necessaria, semper eodem modo se habente.» Cf. Byrne (1968) p. 265.

[54] See *SS* 4, 8: »Primo modo, dicendum est quod certitudo potest considerari dupliciter. Uno modo, ex causa certitudinis, et sic dicitur esse certius quod habet certiorem causam. Et hoc modo fides est certior tribus praedictis (sapientia, scientia, intellectus), quia fides innititur veritati divinae, tria autem praedicta innititur rationi humanae. Alio modo potest considerari certitudo ex parte uitur intellectus hominis. Et per hunc modum, quia ea quae sunt fidei sunt supra intellectum hominis, non autem ea quae subsunt tribus praedictis, ideo ex hac parte fides est minus certa.»

Firstly, it is quite trivial that taken from the viewpoint of the certainty of cause (i.e. ontologically) the condition of truth for certainty is valid: what is objectively and ontologically certain is, of course, true. But how can a man be subjectively certain of what is objectively certain? St. Thomas seems to combine these two certainties with the help of the effect of the First Cause as Final Cause. Where the Final Cause is at work man cannot err from what is objectively certain.[55] This is, as we well know, the function of grace. Therefore, it is grace as a supernatural causality which is needed for a man to be subjectively certain; without grace man may perform a wrong act of faith i.e. assent to the contradictory of what is objectively certain. We see that there is no waterproof acceptance of the condition of truth for the certainty of faith, only there is a tendency to analyse the certainty of faith under the aspect of finality.

Could a man be wholly independent in his certainty of faith from the rational certainty of proof? If the answer is in the affirmative, then there would be an interesting transitive construction in the logic of certainty:

(17) $V_a p \supset V_a V_a p$

This formula would hold, no doubt, for any rational certainty, but not for a combined one.[56] Would it hold for a certainty of faith, too? If so, then some undesirable consequences would follow: If a man were certain by faith of something then he would also be certain by faith of his

---

[55] See *De ver.* 6, 3: (The First Truth) »quando causa infallibiliter effectum producit»; *PP* 82, 1: ». . . sicut intellectus ex necessitate inhaeret primis principiis, ita voluntas ex necessitate inhaeret ultimo fini, qui est beatitudo»; *PP* 5, 2 ad 1: »Bonum autem, cum habeat rationem appetibilis, importat habitudinem causae finalis: cuius causalitas prima est, quia agens non agit nisi propter finem, et agente materia movetur ad forman: unde dicitur quod finis est *causa causarum»; In XII libr. metaph.* V, lectio 2; *PP* 105, 5: »Primo quidem, secundum rationem finis. Cum enim omnis operatio sit propter aliquod bonum verum vel apparens; nihil autem est vel apparet bonum, nisi secundum quod participat aliquam similitudinem summi boni, quod est Deus; sequitur quod ipse Deus sit cuiuslibet operationis causa ut finis.»

[56] See H. Kirjavainen, *Certainty, Assent and Belief.* An Introduction to the Logical and Semantical Analysis of Some Epistemic and Doxastic Notions Especially in the Light of Jaakko Hintikka's Epistemic Logic and Cardinal John Henry Newman's Discussion on Certitude. Publications of the Luther-Agricola-Society B 11, Helsinki 1978, p. 61.

certainty. This is odd and I do not think that St. Thomas would accept it. Rather he would in this case accept an intransitivity principle

(18) $\quad V'_a p \ \& \sim V_a V'_a p.$

It is clear that an intransitive construction like in (18) is suitable for a combined notion of certainty, but at the cost of the two notions of certainty tending to slide apart from each other and so becoming conceptually independent notions. As we already saw, this was precisely what was explicated by St. Thomas when he said that a person could be absolutely certain of something (on the basis of its certain cause) and not be certain (on the basis of proof) that he is certain in that way. Some support also comes from St. Thomas' view on mental acts: if a person performs an act of certainty, he thereby does not necessarily commit himself to carrying out another act of certainty, namely an act which would have the first act as its object. This is because the certainty of mental acts did not have such an important epistemological role for St. Thomas as it had later for nominalist scholastics.

8.11 The condition of justification

We have seen that (K_r) represents a very weak notion of knowledge but that St. Thomas strengthens it so that it satisfies the classical condition

(2) $\quad K_a p \supset J_a p.$

According to St. Thomas (2) is applied to scientific knowledge, but there are also intuitive principles which are either undemonstrable or demonstrable in some higher or more general science.[57]

Formula (2) could be interpreted as saying that if there are no more such possibilities left which could destroy our claim of knowledge, then we have justified knowledge. But this is to identify the condition of justification and the condition of transitivity, because if nothing (in the logical sense) can destroy the claim of knowledge, then it follows that while knowing one simultaneously knows that he knows or at least is in

---

[57] Justification of knowledge is in demonstration. See *PS* 10, 2, ad 3; *In I Post. anal.* I, 44, 402; *De ver.* 11, 1; 8, 4 ad 12.

the position to know that he knows. The condition of transitivity could be formulated as

(19) $K_a p \supset K_a K_a p$.

Did St. Thomas accept (19)? There is at least one crucial problem to be handled before an answer can be given, namely, the problem of *genus* of knowledge. If, as I said in the beginning, the cases of knowing are always acts, then it seems somewhat doubtful whether (19) would hold. This would be for the same reasons as in the case of certainty above, namely, that acts in general are not transitive. Because St. Thomas included the condition of justification into scientific assent and assent is always an act, it seems that St. Thomas did not unrestrictedly accept (19). Typically St. Thomas thinks that there are two different and independent acts involved in cases like (19): knowing of the first order and reflected knowing of the second order. Nevertheless, he seems to think that if we have an act of demonstrative knowledge then we need not repeat the act, and then, by implication this one act is enough for a person to know that he knows.[58] But under the interpretation of intellectual habit (or propositional attitude, as it were) (19) would hold according to St. Thomas, too.

Opinion or weak belief lacks conclusive grounds; it concerns an immediate but contingent proposition.[59] Faith is different. In a certain sense it has grounds because it has an »inner cause» *(causa interiora)*. St. Thomas does not explain very throughly the nature of this cause. Its role, however, is clear enough; it is the light illuminating the mind through revelatory truths. As we saw earlier it is the will which is the decisive moving factor for achieving supernatural truths. Now, St. Thomas wants to say that will is not to be identified with the »inner cause», which is God.

> As to assent to matters of faith, we can look to two types of cause. One is a cause that persuades from without, e.g. a miracle witnessed or a human appeal urging belief. No such cause is enough, however; one man believes and another does not, when both have seen the same miracle, heard the same preaching. Another kind of cause must therefore be present, an inner cause, one that influences a person inwardly to assent to the things of faith. . . . The assent of

---

[58] See *PP* 85, 2; compare *PS* 52, 3.
[59] See *In I Post. anal.* I, 44, 399.

faith, which is its principal act, therefore, has as its cause God, moving us inwardly through grace.[60]

This »inner cause» is not in contradiction with the freedom of will since it is an »inner» forcing factor, not a factor forcing from outside, which would be the criterion for the servitude of the will. Again we see how God as the Final Cause affects the will through grace. Now, if our hypothesis of the implicit teleology holds, then we will get the following result: St. Thomas says in so many words that the knower and the known are the same and that the bridge between them is the similarity. Analogically he says that the virtue of love *somehow* unites the lover and the loved.[61] If the »inner cause» makes us assent to the supernatural truths, it is, at the same time, *the cause and the reason* (or ground) of faith. And if so, then the »inner cause» is simply illuminating divine light, that is to say, an epistemically relevant justification factor.

If the explanation above is correct then St. Thomas proceeds on the same lines as St. Augustine; he accepts the condition

(2') $B^{faith}{}_a p \supset J_a p$.

One problem is that '$J_a p$' does not seem to imply to any argumentative construction at all. It is rather, as in St. Augustine, some kind of insight coming from faith by a substitutive conceptual structure like in (B/K). In this sense it provides to the intellect an answer to the question whether a proposition of faith is true as well as to the question how we can know its truth. Because of the latter answer faith seems to entail a primitive role of justification; being an insight faith satisfies the condition of justification through itself.

---

[60] *SS* 6, 1: »Quantum vero ad secundum, scilicet ad assensum hominis in ea quae sunt fidei, potest considerari duplex causa. Una quidem exterius inducens, sicut miraculum visum, vel persuasio hominis inducentis as fidem. Quorum neutrum est sufficiens causa; videntium enim unum et idem miraculum, et audientium eandem praedicationem, quidam credunt et quidam non credunt. Et ideo oportet ponere aliam causam interiorem, quae movet hominem interius ad assentiendum his quae sunt fidei. . . . Et ideo fides quantum ad assensum, qui est principalis actus fidei, est a Deo interius movente per gratiam.»

[61] See *PS* 28, 1 ad 3: »Ad tertium dicendum quod cognitio perficitur per hoc quod cognitum unitur cognoscenti secundum suam similitudinem. Sed amor facit quod ipsa res quae amatur, amanti aliquo modo uniatur, ut dictum est. Unde amor est magis unitivus quam cognitio.»

But St. Thomas does not want to say that faith somehow provides the intellect with missing syllogistic premisses. Therefore, the »inner cause» does not belong to the area of scientific demonstration at all.

8.12 Simultaneity of faith and knowledge

If knowledge and faith were equivalent they were compatible and could also be temporally simultaneous on purely conceptual grounds. Knowledge and faith would be equivalent, if they would satisfy the same metalogical criteria. St. Thomas explicitly rejects the possibility of simultaneous knowledge and belief, as I said in the outset, because a man cannot at the same time see and not see the same thing. Therefore, the same metalogical criteria are not satisfied by knowledge and faith either. But as we have seen this is not absolutely   ie because St. Thomas, depending on qualifications, both accepts and rejects the formulas

$$(3) \qquad K_ap \supset B_ap$$

and

$$(4) \qquad B_ap \supset K_ap.$$

As such they are not valid formulas in St. Thomas' epistemic logic. If they were valid together, knowledge and faith were conceptually equivalent. This is not, however, the case. On the contrary we see how the qualifications point in different directions.

The following qualifications are made by St. Thomas: firstly, faith does satisfy the condition of truth in the sense of being caused by an infallible cause, thus actualizing its object. Secondly, faith does imply some kind of knowledge, namely, preliminary understanding in the sense of anticipation of informing (*praelibatio*). Thirdly, faith does not properly satisfy the condition of justification; it is neither "seeing" nor demonstration, compared with knowledge it differs in objects. Fourthly, faith, however, has a kind of vindication in the "inner cause". All these qualifications can be explained from the background of implicit teleology because the end is always implicitly present in the cognitive acts, thus building the essential conceptual connections between knowledge and faith.

The only possibility, then, is that knowledge and faith *tend to satisfy the same or similar metalogical criteria without fully succeeding*. This is to say that by assimilation or by conceptual readjustments they tend to have a similar conceptual role. But this means that they tend to become similar *in intension* or *as concepts,* not as explicitly simultaneous states of mind or propositional attitudes

The main conclusion is that although St. Thomas explicitly rejects the simultaneity of faith and knowledge, in some sense, partly from implicit reasons, he qualifies faith in such a way that his rejection will become somewhat diluted. Faith is simultaneous with knowledge by being a kind of knowledge, the »light of faith« as it were. This, of course, is the old Augustinian tendency for clearing a place for faith on the map of epistemic notions.

So far it seems obvious that St. Thomas did in the main accept the classical definition of knowledge, but the condition of belief (3) was the principal source of trouble. Because faith in its core is an act as well as an attitude, the notion of assent becomes very important. Its main function is to transmit the conceptual structure of effective action into faith. On behalf of implicit teleology this structure appears to be a conceptual connection between the objects of faith and the end of will. Therefore, the role of assent heavily supports the assimilation of the metalogical criteria of faith with the metalogical criteria of knowledge, because assent is qualified in a theological context by absolute certainty and directedness to eternal, though contingent objects. On behalf of influence of assent faith becomes a type of a wedge between scientific knowledge and mere belief or opinion. Its truths cannot be achieved once and for all by a single act of assent, but by repeated acts. Therefore the model of faith in St. Thomas could perhaps be called a »knocking on the door« model of faith. Cognitive perfection *(visio Dei)* can be achieved by faith only by the soul's voluntary and repeated assents. In this way the tendency of the assimilation of metalogical criteria can be explained. But complete assimilation is not possible; faith still remains epistemically a weaker notion than knowledge. Faith always needs some »auxiliary concepts«, e.g. that of grace, in order to reach the metalogical level of knowledge.

Our other questions at the outset can also be answered now: as to the difference between different epistemic faculties on the basis of different objects, it is to be said that it holds for St. Thomas, too. As to the nature of the objects of faith and knowledge, it is to be said that they are mainly *enuntiationes* (i.e. meanings) propositions, but also, in some very important cases of faith, objects of acquaintances in the sense of *praelibationes*.

So we see that it is somewhat misleading to think that St. Thomas represented a theory in which faith is epistemically on a par with knowledge. In this sense e.g. the view of Karl Rahner is incorrect although Rahner's interpretation could become correctly theorized as a »logic of being aware» instead of the logic of knowledge. Rather St. Thomas' epistemic logic is to be explained on the basis of implicit teleology, which cause the pressure for accepting criteria which make faith to act like a wedge between knowledge and belief. If this is correct then St. Thomas is a culmination of the tendencies that began with Plato, Aristotle and St. Augustine. But essentially he did not step outside the basic conceptual presuppositions of those tendencies.

9. CONCLUSION

We started from the so-called classical definition of knowledge and sketched the classical difference between knowledge and belief. The decisive trait was that knowledge and belief have different objects: eternal versus temporal. Different objects suffice to make them mutually exclusive faculties from which it follows that knowledge and belief cannot exist simultaneously in the same person directed to the same object.

One of the roots of the conceptual difficulties was the ambivalent attitude of Plato towards the formula

$$(3) \qquad K_a p \supset B_a p.$$

This ambivalence in turn had its background in the discrepancy between intensional and extensional analysis of forms in Plato's theory of ideas. The same ambivalence goes through the history of epistemic logic until the Middle Ages.

From the days of St. Augustine the need for a peculiar epistemic notion has been apparent. A notion which would be compatible with the criteria expressed in the classical definition of knowledge, but which would also satisfy the needs of religious faith was perpetually proposed and discussed by theologians. The tendencies which were proposed can be described as follows:

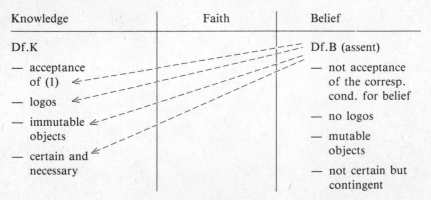

Knowledge	Faith	Belief
Df.K		Df.B (assent)
— acceptance of (1)		— not acceptance of the corresp. cond. for belief
— logos		— no logos
— immutable objects		— mutable objects
— certain and necessary		— not certain but contingent

By this diagram we can easily outline the historical development of epistemic notions. Somewhat roughly we could state that the history of western epistemic thought shows that religious faith is to be understood neither as pure knowledge nor as pure belief (or opinion), but something between. The propositions as objects of faith are neither properly known nor properly believed, but assented to with full certainty. Interestingly enough, this solution does not yet totally imply that faith would be something *sui generis* in any modern sense of an autonomy of religious language. Nevertheless, the solution does imply a seed for it.

A part of these problematics is due to the fact that the linguistic construction of faith is until the Middle Ages mainly that of 'knowing that' or 'believing that' i.e. the construction for propositional attitudes. Because 'knowing how' is not thoroughly reducible to 'knowing that', we may say that there is a real conceptual prevalence of the propositional faith at expence of the non-propositional one. Partly this is due to the difference between faith as act and faith as attitude. How this difference is best explained historically is a matter that we have tried to clarify. Similarly the central role of knowledge by acquaintance beginning from antiquity can also be seen from the point of view of two linguistic constructions: 'knowing who' and 'knowing that'. How far is faith constructed as acquaintance, and how far is it propositional? We have seen, I hope, that the answer to this question is that the inner nature of faith as acquaintance is, nevertheless, expressed in western theology and philosophy mainly by the notion of assenting to something. Because this assenting to something is in favor of the propositional view as well as of the acquaintance-view there is no sharp distinction between the significations of the two constructions.

ABBREVIATIONS

CC   = Corpus Christianorum
CSEL   = Corpus scriptorum ecclesiaticorum latinorum
LGEMP = The Cambridge History of Later Greek and Early Medieval Philosophy
LMP   = The Cambridge History of Later Medieval Philosophy
PG   = Migne, Patrologia Graeca
PL   = Migne, Patrologia Latina
PP   = St. Thomas Aquinas, Summa Theologiae, Pars Prima
PS   = *ibid*. Prima Secundae
SS   = *ibid*. Secunda Secundae
TP   = *ibid*. Tertia Pars

SOURCES AND LITERATURE

Albert the Great,
1890—99   Summa Theologiae, De Intellectu et Intelligibili, Opera omnia. Ed. A
            Borgnet, Paris.

Alexander of Aphrodisias,
1883   In Aristotelis De anima commentarium. Ed. M. Wallies, *Commentaria
            in Aristotelem Graeca.*

St. Anselm of Canterbury,
1946—61   S. Anselmi Cantuariensis Archiepiscopi Opera Omnia. Ed. F. S. Schmitt,
            O.S.B., Edinburgh.
            — De veritate, Vol. I,
            — Cur Deus Homo, Vol. II.

1965   Proslogion, with a Reply on Behalf of the Fool by Gaunilo and The
            Author's Reply to Gaunilo, Transl. M. J. Charlesworth, Text and
            Translation, Oxford *(PL* 158).

Aristotle,
1973   Aristotle in Twenty-Three Volumes, *Loeb Classical Library,* Ed. E. H.
            Warmington, Cambridge, Mass. — London.
            — Categories, Vol. I,
            — Posterior Analytics, Vol. II,
            — Topics, Vol. II,
            — On Sophistical Refutations, Vol. III,
            — Physics, Vol. IV and V,
            — On the Soul, Vol. VIII,
            — Metaphysics, Vol. XVIII,
            — Nicomachean Ethics, Vol. IX,

St. Augustine,
1957   Corpus christianorum, (= *CC),* Series latina, Avrelii Avgvstini opera,
            Tvrnholti.
            — Confessiones, Vol. XXVII,
            — Contra Academicos, Vol. XXIX,
            — De Ordine, Vol. XXIX,
            — De Magistro, Vol. XXIX,
            — De Libero Arbitrio, Vol. XXIX,

— In Johannis Euangelium Tractatus, Vol. XXXVI,
— Enarrationes in Psalmos, Vol. XXXVIII—XL,
— Enchiridion, Vol. XLVI,
— De Diversis Questionibus, Vol. XLIV,
— De Civitate Dei, Vol. XLVII—XLVIII,
— De Trinitate, Vol. L—L$_A$,
Corpus Scriptorum Ecclesiasticorum Latinorum *(= CSEL)*.
— Epistolas, Vol. 34, 44, 57, 58,
— Retractationes, Vol. 36,
— De Spiritu et Littera, Vol. 60,
Patrologia latina *(= PL)*.
— De praedestinatione sanctorum Vol. 44,
Des Heiligen Kirchenvaters Aurelius Augustinus Ausgewählte Briefe. Übers. von A Hoffmann, *Bibliothek der Kirchenväter* IX, München, Letter 120, p. 462—481.

Bacon, Roger,
1897—1900   Opus majus. J. H. Bridges, Williams and Norgate, Clarendon Press, Oxford.

1905—1940   Quaestiones supra libros quatuor Physicorum, Opera hactenus inedita Fratris Rogeri Baconis, 16 vols., Ed. R. Steele, Oxford.

Beierwaltes, W.,
1963   »Der Begriff 'unum in nobis' bei Proklos», Die Metaphysik im Mittelalter. Miscellanea medievalia, Band 2, Berlin, p. 255—266.

Boethius,
1957   Anicii Manlii Severini Boethii Philosophiae consolatio. Ed. L. Bieler, Turnholt *(CC* XCIV).

1969   Commentarii in librum Aristotelis Analytica Priora. *Aristoteles latinus* III, Ed. Minio-Paluello, Leiden *(PL* 64).

1978   De topiciis differentiis. Ed. E. Stump, Cornell.
            De Hebdomadibus *(PL* 64).

St. Bonaventura,
1883—1902   Opera omnia. Ed. PP. collegi a S. Bonaventura, Quaracchi.
            — In quattuor libros sententiarum, Vol. I—IV,
            — Quaestiones disputatae, Vol. V, (De scientia Christi, De mysterio Trinitatis),
            — Breviloquium, Vol. V,
            — Opusculum de reductione artium ad theologiam, Vol. V,
            — Itinerarium mentis in Deum, Vol. V.

Byrne, E. F.,
1968   Probability and Opinion. A Study in the Medieval Presuppositions of Post-Medieval Theories of Probability. The Hague.

The Cambridge History of Later Greek and Early Medieval Philosophy. Ed. A. H.
1967   Armstrong, Cambridge *(LGEMP).*

The Cambridge History of Later Medieval Philosophy from the Rediscovery of
1982   Aristotle to the Disintegration of Scholasticism 1100—1600. Eds. N.
              Kretzmann, A. Kenny, J. Pinborg, E. Stump, Cambridge, London, New
              York, New Rochelle, Melbourne, Sydney *(LMP).*

Chadwick, Henry,
1981   Boethius. The Consolations of Music, Logic, Theology, and Philosophy.
              Oxford.

Gersh, Stephen,
1978   From Iamblichus to Eriugena. An Investigation of the Prehistory and
              Evolution of the Pseudo-Dionysian Tradition. Leiden.

Gilbert of Poitiers,
1966   The Commentaries on Boethius by Gilbert of Poitiers. Ed. N. M.
              Häring, Pontifical Institute of Mediaeval Studies *(PL* 64).

Grabmann, Martin,
1911   Die Geschichte der scholastischen Methode. Freiburg im Breisgau.

Gregory of Nyssa,
              Contra Eunomium *(PG* 45).

Grosseteste, Robert,
1912   Die philosophischen Werke des Robert Grosseteste zum ersten Mal
              vollständig in kritischer Ausgabe besorgt von L. Baur, Münster.
              — De Lineis, Angulis et Figuris,
              — Commentaria in Libros Posteriorum Analyticorum Aristotelis.

Hare, R. M.,
1982   Plato. Oxford.

Henry, D. P.,
1972   Medieval Logic and Metaphysics. London.

Hintikka, Jaakko,
1962   Knowledge and Belief. An Introduction to the Logic of the Two Notions.
              Ithaca, New York.

1974   Knowledge and the Known. Historical Perspectives in Epistemology.
              Synthese Historical Library 11, Dordrecht-Holland/Boston-U.S.A.
              »Knowledge and its Objects in Plato», *ibid.* p. 1—30.

1975   »Different Constructions in Terms of the Basic Epistemological Verbs»,
              The Intentions of Intentionality and Other New Models for Modalities.
              Synthese Library 90, Dordrecht-Holland/Boston-U.S.A.

John of Salisbury,
1929   Metalogicon libri 4. Ed. C. C. J. Webb, Oxford *(PL* 199).

Kenny, Anthony,
1980   Aquinas. Oxford.

Kirjavainen, Heikki,
1978   Certainty, Assent and Belief. An Introduction to the Logical and Semantical Analysis of Some Epistemic and Doxastic Notions Especially in the Light of Jaakko Hintikka's Epistemic Logic and Cardinal John Henry Newman's Discussion on Certitude. *Publications of Luther-Agricola-Society* B 11, Helsinki.

1983   Uskon ja tiedon samanaikaisuus. Totuus-, perustelu- ja varmuusehdon esiintymisiä uskonnollisen uskon määrittelyssä antiikista korkeaskolastiikkaan. (The Simultaneity of Faith and Knowledge. The Conditions of Truth, Justification and Certainty in the Definitions of Religious Belief from Antiquity to High Scholasticism). *Publications of the Finnish Society of Theological Literature* 137, Helsinki.

Kneale, William and Martha,
1966   The Development of Logic. Oxford.

Knudsen, Christian,
1982   »Intentions and Impositions», *LMP.*

Knuuttila, Simo,
1981   »Time and Modality in Scholasticism», Reforging the Great Chain of Being. Studies of the History of Modal Theories. Ed. S. Knuuttila, *Synthese Historical Library* 20, Dordrecht-Holland/Boston-U.S.A./London-England.

1982   »Modal Logic», LMP.

Kuksewicz, Z.,
1982   »The Potential and Agent Intellect», *LMP* p. 595—601.

Lang, Albert,
1964   Die theologische Prinzipienlehre der mittelalterlichen Scholastik. Freiburg—Basel—Wien.

Leff, Gordon,
1958   Medieval Thought. London.

Lenzen, Wolfgang,
1978   Recent Work in Epistemic Logic. *Acta Philosophica Fennica.* Vol. 30, No. 1, Amsterdam.

Liebschütz, H.,
1968   »Boethius and the Legacy of Antiquity», *LGEMP,* p. 538—564.
»Anselm of Canterbury: The Philosophical Interpretation of Faith», *LGEMP,* p. 611—639.

Loux, M.,
1978   Substance and Attribute. A Study in Ontology. A Pallas Paperback / 8, Dordrecht-Holland/Boston-U.S.A./London-England.

Lovejoy, Arthur,
1948   The Great Chain of Being. A Study of the History of an Idea. Cambridge, Massachusetts.

de Lubac, Henri,
1946   Surnaturel. Paris.

Maréchal, Joseph,
1947   Le point de depart de la métaphysique V. Le thomisme devant la philosophie critique. Bruxelles.

Markus, R. A.,
1967   »Reason and Illumination», *LGEMP,* p. 362—373.

Maurer, A. A.,
1968   Medieval Philosophy. New York.

Moravcsik, Julius,
1973   »Plato's Method of Division», Patterns in Plato's Thought. Ed. J. Moravcsik, Dordrecht-Holland/Boston-U.S.A.

Murdoch, John,
1982   »Infinity and Continuity», *LMP.*

Nuchelmans, G.,
1973   Theories of the Proposition. Ancient and medieval conceptions of the bearers of truth and falsity. *North-Holland Linguistic Series,* Eds. S. C. Dik and J. G. Kooij, Amsterdam—London.

1981   »The Semantics of Propositions», *LMP,* p. 197—210.

Owens, J.,
1981   »Faith, Ideas, Illumination, and Experience» *LMP,* p. 440—459.

Pinborg, Jan,
1972   Logik und Semantik im Mittelalter. Stuttgart-Bad Canstatt.

Plato,
1950   Platonis opera. Ed. J. Burnet, Oxonii.
            — Theaitetos,
            — Republic,
            — Timaeus,
            — Gorgias.

Plotin,
1966   Enneades. *The Loeb Classical Library,* Ed. A. H. Armstrong, London, Vols. V and VI.

Porphyry,
1887   Isagoge et in Aristotelis Categorias Commentarium. Ed. A. Busse.

Potts, Timothy,
1971   »Aquinas on Belief and Faith», Inquiries into Medieval Philosophy. A Collection in Honor of Francis P. Clarke. Westport, Connecticut.

Proclos,
1963   Elementatio Theologica, Ed. E. R. Dodds, Oxford.

1968   Theologia Platonis, Ed. H. D. Saffrey—L. G. Westerink, Paris.

104

Pseudo-Dionysios,
1947   De divinis nominibus, Enchiridion Patristicum coll. M. J. Rouet de
              Journel, EP 2280/5.
              De mystica theologia, Enchiridion asceticum coll. Rouet de Journel et
              Dutilleul, EA 1044 et al.
              De caelesti hierarchia, EA 1044 et al.

Rahner, Karl,
1941   Hörer des Wortes. Zur Grundlegung einer Religionsphilosophie.
              München.

Ross, Sir David,
1968   Aristotle. University Paperback.

Schmidt, Robert W.,
1966   The Domain of Logic according to St. Thomas Aquinas. The Hague.

St. Thomas Aquinas,
1882   In Libros Posteriorum Analyticorum, Roma.

1929—47   Scriptum in IV Libros Sententiarum. Ed. P. Mandonnet & M. F. Moos,
              Paris.

1949   Quaestiones disputatae, De veritate. Ed. R. M. Spiazzi, Torino.
              In X Libros Ethicorum. Ed. R. M. Spiazzi, Torino.
              Questiones disputatae de Malo. Ed. R. M. Spiazzi, Torino.

1950   In XII libros metaphysicorum. Ed. R. M. Spiazzi, Torino.

1956   Summa Theologiae. Ed. Caramello & Marietti.

Serene, Eileen,
1982   »Demonstrative Science», *LMP,* p. 496—517.

Sheldon-Williams, I. P.,
1967   »St. Gregory of Nyssa», *LGEMP,* p. 447—456.
              »The Pseudo-Dionysios», *LGEMP,* p. 457—472.

van Steenberghen, Ferdinand,
1977   Die Philosophie im 13. Jahrhundert. München—Paderborn—Wien.

Wéber, Edouard-Henri,
1976   »Les discussions de 1270 a l'université de Paris et leur influence sur
              la pense philosophique de S. Thomas d'Aquin», Die Auseinanderset-
              zungen an der Pariser Universität im XIII Jahrhundert. Ed.
              A. Zimmermann, *Miscellanea medievalia,* Band 10, Berlin—New York,
              p. 285—316.

Weisheipl, James A.,
1974   Friar Thomas D'Aquino. His Life, Thought, and Work. Doubleday
              & Company, Inc., Garden City, New York.

William of Auvergne,
1963   De anima. Opera omnia. Orleans and Paris 1674, Reprinted by Minerva.

Wittgenstein, Ludwig,
1933   Tractatus-Logico-Philosophicus.

Wolfson, Harry,
1965   Religious Philosophy: A Group of Essays. Atheneum—New York.

1976   The Philosophy of the Church Fathers. Faith, Trinity, Incarnation.
            Cambridge Mass. and London England.

RISTO SAARINEN

MORAL WEAKNESS AND HUMAN ACTION IN JOHN BURIDAN'S ETHICS

MORAL WEAKNESS AND HUMAN ACTION IN JOHN BURIDAN'S ETHICS

I

Although most of the recent studies on John Buridan concentrate on his logical and scientific writings, the influence of this 14th century Parisian Master of Arts has been of no less importance in the history of ethics. Buridan's *Quaestiones super decem libros Ethicorum* was the standard commentary on Nicomachean Ethics in the European universities until the sixteenth century. The number of extant manuscripts as well as the many early printed editions indicate the great influence of Buridanism in practical philosophy.[1]

The aim of this article is to analyze John Buridan's view on moral weakness (incontinentia, akrasia). The main interest will be directed to the problem of how this view is related to Buridan's conception of human action in general. There are several reasons why the concept of moral weakness or »incontinence» is of special importance when we try to describe the development of late medieval philosophical ethics. To see the relevance of this concept we must examine its history a little closer.

---

[1] On the life and work of John Buridan see E. *Faral,* Jean Buridan: Maître ès arts de l'Universite de Paris', in: Histoire litteraire de la France, vol. 38, 462—605. On the influence on Buridan's commentary cf. J. J. *Walsh,* Buridan and Seneca, Journal of the History of Ideas 27, 1966, 23—25; J. *Korolec,* Filozofia Moralna Jana Burydana, Polska Akademia Nauk. Warzaw 1973; *ibid.,* Le Commentaire de Jean Buridan sur l'Ethique à Nicomaque et l'université de Cracovie dans la première moitié du XV siècle', Organon 10, 1974, 187—208; G. *Wieland.* The Reception and Interpretation of Aristotle's Ethics, in: The Cambridge History of Later Medieval Philosophy (= CHM), ed. N. Kretzmann, A. Kenny, J. Pinborg, Cambridge 1982, 668—670. The editions of Buridan's commentary and secondary literature are listed in CHM; the catalogue of manuscripts is found in *Traditio* 1973, 179—181.

Walsh (1966, 24—25) concludes: »Whatever we find in this commentary we may be sure was available to thousands of students over hundreds of years — just those years when the great transition from medieval to modern thought was being accomplished.»

Aristotle's treatment of moral weakness has recently received a great deal of scholarly interest, especially because incontinent people are, in his opinion, the only group of human beings who seem to be able to behave in opposition to the end result of the calculative reason.[2] Although the reasoning faculty of the incontinent people is not perverted, they cannot follow the voice of right reason and they fail to do good. Incontinence is for Aristotle a philosophical problem, because he is an intellectualist in his action theory: practical reason eliminates all alternatives except the best one, which is then necessarily chosen by a good man. The Aristotelian choice (prohairesis) is therefore not a choice among alternatives. Accordingly, the conclusion of the practical syllogism is the action.[3] But, if no man sins willingly, as Socrates formulated the intellectualist axiom, how is it possible for an incontinent person to possess right reason and yet commit sin? Aristotle argues that the incontinent man does not possess right reason when he acts against it; the right reason can be manifested before and after its conclusion is violated but not at the very moment of violation.[4]

Aristotle's intellectualist view is continuously challenged during the Middle Ages by the Christian theologians who claim that sin is a conscious act of the will. The Christian use of the concepts 'continentia' and 'incontinentia' is primarily related to chastity and celibacy and is already used by St. Paul in the Vulgata (1. Cor. 7: 5, Gal. 5: 23, 2. Tim. 3: 3). St. Augustine and Peter Lombard follow the use of St.Paul.[5] According to Bernhard of Clairvaux, the monastic life is called *ordo continentium*.[6] Martin Luther points out that Jerome related continence to virginity.[7]

---

[2] S. *Knuuttila,* The Emergence of Deontic Logic in the Fourteenth Century, in: R. Hilpinen (ed.), New Studies in Deontic Logic, Dordrecht 1981, 233. Cf. J. J. *Walsh,* Aristotle's Conception of Moral Weakness, New York 1963; W. F. R. *Hardie,* Aristotle's Ethical Theory, Oxford 1968; R. *Robinson,* Aristotle on Akrasia, in: J. Barnes, M. Schefield, R. Sorabji (ed.) Articles on Aristotle 2, Ethics & Politics, London 1977, 79—91.

[3] *Aristotle,* Ethica Nicomachea (=EN) 1147a 26—28; 1111b 5—1112a 17; *Knuuttila* 1981, 233.

[4] EN 1147a 10—1147b 19; *Knuuttila* 1981, 233.

[5] Cf. *Augustine,* Patrol. latina 36,679,52—53 and 34, 399—400 = *Lombard,* Sent. II dist. 20 cap. 1,3; *Lombard,* Sent. IV dist. 31 cap. 7: »Incontinentiae malum est quod vir cognoscit uxorem etiam ultra necessitatem procreandi liberos.«

[6] *Bernhard,* De div. sermo 35 n. 1. Cited in R. *Schwartz,* Vorgeschichte der reformatorischen Busstheologie, Berlin 1968, 97.

[7] *Luther,* Weimarer Ausgabe 40/2, 120, 7—10.

The approach of Aristotelian Scholasticism is, of course, more differentiated. Thomas Aquinas follows Aristotle's interpretation. A virtuous man cannot do anything wrong.[8] That Thomas' solution to the problem of sinning willingly follows the intellectualism of Aristotle can be seen from his exposition of EN 1147 b 9—18. At the moment of sinning the incontinent man »non possit in actu scire», because a passion has obscured the singular term of the practical syllogism.[9] The same view can be found in *Summa Theologiae* (II/II q 156 a 1). Sin is therefore due to ignorance temporarily caused by passion.

Contrary to Thomas's view, the Franciscan *Correctorium fratris Thomae* defends the view that a person's will can consciously act against the reason. The Correctorium follows Walter Brugge's solutions to the problem of incontinence. Walter in opposition to Aristotle declares that an incontinent person can be fully aware of the fact that his action is deviant.[10] The voluntaristic view of John Duns Scotus and the Franciscans in general differs significantly from the Aristotelian-Thomistic conception. William of Ockham also prefers the voluntaristic interpretation of moral weakness by emphasizing the freedom of the will in its choice. The will of a continent man can »ex libertate sua» conquer concupiscence; accordingly, the will of an incontinent person will freely follow (vult libere sequi) concupiscence.[11] Although the most influential in-

---

[8] *Knuuttila* 1981, 233—234.

[9] Thomas *Aquinas,* Sententia libri Ethicorum, lib. VII, 1c 3, n. 25 (ed. Marietti 1949, 363): »Deinde cum dicit 'quia autem'. Secundum praemissa solvit rationem Socratis. Et dicit, quod propositio et opinio ultima, scilicet singularis, accipitur per sensum et principatur in actionibus quae sunt circa singularia. Huiusmodi autem propositionem aut opinionem ille qui est in passione vel omnino non habet habitum vel habet habitum ligatum, ut non possit in actu scire, sed hoc modo loquitur de his, sicut ebrius dicit verba Empedoclis. Quia ergo ista sunt vera, et quia universale quod per scientiam comprehenditur non est extremus terminus operabilium, videtur sequi illud quod Socrates quaerebat. Patet enim ex predictis, quod passio non sit in praesentia principalis scientiae quae est circa universale, quum passio sit solum in particulari. Neque univeralis scientia trahitur a passione, sed solum existimatio sensibilis quae non est tantae dignitatis.»

[10] E. *Stadter,* Psychologie und Metaphysik der menschlichen Freiheit. Die ideengeschichtliche Entwicklung zwischen Bonaventura und Duns Scotus. Paderborn 1971, 78—81, 243—244. *William de la Mare,* Correctorium 331—333 (cited in *Stadter* 1971).

[11] *Guillelmi de Ockham* Quaestiones variae, Opera theologica VIII, St. Bonaventure, N.Y. 1984, 272, 280—281: »quia continens est ille qui habet concupiscentias

terpretations of moral weakness are sketched above in a very simplified form, it can be maintained that the differences in the interpretation reflect the acceptance or refutation of the Aristotelian psychology of human action. If it is supposed that the formal cause of human choice is reason and the material cause the will — as Thomas Aquinas defines it — »the will cannot will anything else than what is put on it as its form by the reason».[12] Consequently, the passion which leads an incontinent man to the deviant action is not seen as one possible choice among others but as an affect which directly obscures the actual knowledge of the practical syllogism. This intellectualist interpretation is defended by the scholars of via antiqua, whereas the *moderni* preferred a voluntaristic view according to which the will of an incontinent man can consciously act against his reason.

John Buridan's extensive treatment of incontinence in the seventh book of his commentary can thus help us in defining his philosophical position between the traditions of via antiqua and via moderna. Although it is often argued that Buridan was »the leading Parisian follower of William of Ockham»[13], it is also well known that many traditions of via antiqua are continued in Buridan's Commentary on Ethics.[14] Recent scholarly work has shown that in several questions Buridan has found an original way of solving the problem and has carefully avoided the

---

pravas, tamen non sequit eas, sed sequitur rectam rationem secundum Philosophum. Quod sic intelligo quod continens est ille qui apprehendit aliqua obiecta delectabilia et appetit illa appetitu sensitivo. Sed recta ratio dictat contrarium illius quod est desideratum ab appetitu sensitivo. Et voluntas ex libertate sua non vult illud quod desiderat appetitus sensitivus, sed illud quod est dictatum a recta ratione, ita quod respectu illius volitionis recta ratio est obiectum partiale sicut alibi patet.»

»Eodem modo est dicendum de habitibus oppositis predictis tribus quos ponit Philosophus ibi, qui sunt incontinentia, malitia et bestialitas. Quia incontinentia, prout reperitur in voluntate, est habitus quo aliquis habens concupiscentias pravas dimittit rectam rationem et vult libere sequi concupiscentias illas.»

[12] *Thomas Aquinas,* Summa theol. II/I q 1, q 13 a 1. *Knuuttila* 1981, 234.

[13] J. J. *Walsh,* Some Relationships between Gerald Odo's and John Buridan's Commentaries on Aristotle's Ethics, Franciscan Studies 35, 1975, 246.

[14] Cf. *Walsh* 1966, 1975, *Walsh,* Nominalism and the Ethics: Some Remarks about Buridan's Commentary, Journal of the History of Philosophy 4, 1966, 1—13; *ibid.,* Is Buridan a Skeptic about Free Will, Vivarium 2, 1964, 50—61; *ibid.,* Teleology in the Ethics of Buridan, Journal of the History of Philosophy 1980, 265—286; CHM, 667—668.

shortcomings of Thomism and Ockhamism. Because of the great influence of Buridan's Commentary it is worth studying if that is also the case in his treatment of incontinence and human action. In the following we shall use the text of the 1513 edition.[15]

In Book III, quest. 1—5 the conceptual background for the treatment of incontinence is formulated. Although these questions have already been studied by scholars[16], there are still some interesting points to be made in connection with human action and moral weakness. Therefore we begin (II) by analyzing some central ideas in these questions. Subsequently (III) the role of incontinence in Buridan's action theory can be examined. In the last part of the article (IV) a conclusive summary of the results is presented.

II

The first question in Book III is formulated as follows: »Whether it is possible for the will, with everything else disposed the same way, to be determined sometimes to one of the opposites and sometimes to the other?»[17] Scholars have paid attention to Buridan's final answer to the question, because Buridan concludes that we must believe this »freedom of opposition» because of faith and moral responsibility, even though we cannot present sufficient rational grounds for this kind of freedom.[18]

---

[15] *Johannes Buridanus,* Super decem libros Ethicorum, Paris 1513. Unveränderter Nachdruck, Frankfurt 1968. According to *Walsh* (1980, 266) this edition is »an excellent piece of work». For the manuscripts, editions and studies cf. the literature given in footnotes 1, 13, 14 and E. J. *Monahan,* Human Liberty and Free Will according to John Buridan, Medieval Studies XVI, 1954, 72—86; J. *Korolec,* Les principes de la philosophie morale de Jean Buridan. Medievalia philosophica Polonarum 21, 1975, 53—72.

As *Walsh* 1975 has shown, Buridan supplies extensive quotations and reminiscences from Gerald Odo in his commentary. None of the texts analyzed in this paper is, however, influenced by Odo's commentary.

[16] Cf. *Monahan* 1954, *Walsh* 1964 and *Korolec* 1973.

[17] *Buridan,* op.cit. 36rb: »Utrum sit possibile quod voluntas, ceteris omnibus eodem modo se habentibus, determinetur aliquando ad unum oppositorum, aliquando ad aliud?»

This kind of freedom is in the following referred to as the »freedom of opposition».

[18] Cf. *Monahan* 1954 and *Walsh* 1964 passim; *Walsh* 1980, 279.

Whether this solution is an expression of resignation or skepticism, does not interest us in this connection. It is more important to see which are the central arguments presented by Buridan for and against this freedom. To find out the crucial points in Buridan's extensive treatment we must begin by presenting an outline of the argumentation as a whole.

1. The Question. (fol. 36 rb)
2. Argument quod sic. (36 rb)
3. Argument quod non. (36 rb)
4. A new formulation: Whether the act of the will is necessarily determined by its object or by something else? (36 rb)
5. An opinio communis: The ultimate end of this act is necessarily determined but the will can choose between the different means and ways to that end. (36 rb—va)
6. Arguments for opinio communis:
6.1. It is shown by experience. (36 va)
6.2. Otherwise the will would not be free. (36 va)
6.3. Otherwise we would not be masters of our own acts. (36 va)
6.4. Otherwise there would be neither merit nor sin. (36 va)
7. Arguments against opinio communis:
7.1. Critique of the argument 6.4. (36 va—vb)
7.2. The action can be explained as an actualization of a sufficient disposition. Therefore we need not postulate an additional free will as agent. (36 vb—37 ra)
7.3. Choosing between two possibilities stands in contradiction with the axiom »omnia generabile generabitur». (37 ra—rb)
7.4. Refutation of the arguments 6.1—6.4. (37 rb)
8. The solution: Because of faith and moral responsibility we must believe the freedom of will to be determined sometimes to one of the opposites and sometimes to the other. (37 rb—va)
9. Refutation of the arguments presented in 7. (37 va—vb)
10. Refutation of the argument presented in 3. (37 vb)

The crucial point of the question is whether a negative answer would inevitably lead to determinism. The idea of argument 2. is to show that in order to preserve the freedom of the will the a positive answer to the question must be given. The freedom of the will means that the will is not necessitated to choose either of the opposites and it is argued that this is not the case if the negative answer is preferred.[19]

On the contrary, it is argued for the *quod non* position that the

---

[19] *Buridan,* op.cit. 36 rb: »Et arguitur quod sic, quia aliter ipsa voluntas non esset libera, quod est inconveniens. Consequentia patet, quia ex alio non dicitur libera, nisi quia ad neutrum oppositorum est necessitata, modo ipsa semper, scilicet in quodlibet instanti, esset ad alterum necessitata, quia res omnes in eodem instanti se habent eodem modo; aliter enim et aliter se habere est in alio et alio instanti, nisi contradic-

freedom of opposition couldn't exist even though the will weren't yet determined towards either of the opposites. In such case the will would always be either equally determined to both opposites or more determined to one than another. If the will is equally determined towards both alternatives, it can never be determined but always defers its act. If the will is more determined to a than b, it can never be determined to b. In both cases the freedom of opposition is regarded as impossible because it never occurs.[20]

According to both positions determination can be avoided only if the possibility of the will to defer its act without determination to any given alternative is preserved. It is well known that Buridan's conception of free will largely consists of the will's power of deferring its act.[21] Both sides, *quod sic* and *quod non,* agree with this definition. The real problem is whether there are such cases in which the will is able to defer its act so that it can afterwards become determined to both opposites. If not, then »the act of the will is necessarily determined by its object or by something else», as the new formulation of the question says (4.). By re-formulating the question in this way Buridan intends to define the cases in which the will can defer its act without being immediately necessitated »by its object or by something else». These cases, as we shall see, constitute the range of possibilities to which the freedom of opposition refers. To see how Buridan reaches this definition we must first look closer at the determinist arguments in 7.2. and 7.3.

---

toria concedantur simul esse vera. Sed tu ponis quod rebus aliis omnibus eodemmodo se habentibus ipsa non potest ad opposita determinari, sed solum ad alterum oppositorum. Ergo in quolibet instanti ipsa ad alterum oppositorum necessitatur.»

[20] 36 rb: »Oppositum arguitur: quia in isto nunc, secundum quod res se habet, vel voluntas est indifferens omnino ad utrumque oppositorum vel magis est determinata ad unum quam ad alterum, quamvis non concederetur simpliciter determinata. Si primo modo, tunc videtur quod rebus sic stantibus ipsa numquam sic determinaretur. Probatio: quia qua ratione determinaretur ad hoc, eadem ratione ad illud; aut ergo ad utrumque, quod est impossibile, nisi concedas opposita simul verificari, aut ad neutrum et habetur intentum. . . . Si autem voluntas fuerit ad unam partem magis determinata et inclinata et ad aliam minus, verbi gratia, sit magis determinata ad a et minus ad b, tunc rebus sic se habentibus nunquam determinabitur ad b, quoniam minus se habet ad b, quam si esset indifferens equaliter ad a et ad b. Et tamen si esset indifferens, non determinaretur, ut dictum est. Ergo multo minus poterit nunc determinari ad b.»

[21] Cf. for example *Monahan* 1954; *Korolec* 1973, 1975.

Argument 7.2 asserts that all action can be explained as actualizations of passive potencies which have reached a state of sufficient disposition. If all necessary conditions are fulfilled, the action necessarily begins; no additional act of the will is needed.[22] Buridan refutes this argument by introducing a distinction between natural and voluntary agents and by saying that the argument is not valid in the case of voluntary agents.[23] It follows a long series of counter-arguments and the theme is continued in the second question of Book III. It is not necessary to follow this lengthy dispute here; for our purposes it is enough to mention that the original distinction is maintained and the will is finally given a partial activity in the process of action, as we shall see a little later in our analysis.

Argument 7.3. tries to make Aristotle a determinist by using his axiom »omnia generabile generabitur». If something is assumed to be possible, then no impossibility follows when this possibility is realized. In accordance with this definition of possibility it can be maintained that a thing capable of generating will generate. If we assume that something capable of generating would not generate, this assumption would stand in contradiction with the fact that this thing, because it is capable of generating, will generate.[24] The same contradiction follows from assuming the freedom of opposition. If the will is simultaneously able to will (velle)

---

[22] 36 vb: »Contra tamen hanc opinionem fortiter arguitur: quia agente sufficienter approximato passo sufficienter disposito, et in illa dispositione sufficiente, in qua alterum innatum est agere et alterum pati, oportet quod fiat actio, quam hoc est innatum agere et illud pati. Sed si rebus stantibus, ut nunc stant, ego sine alio determinante possum velle agere, tunc omnia posita sunt requisita ad hunc actum, qui est velle legere; ergo necessario ponetur velle legere.»

[23] 36 vb.

[24] 37 ra: »Item Aristoteles et Commentator, primo Celi et Mundi, et in nono Methaphysice capitulo illo: 'sunt autem alii ut megarici', videtur expresse velle quod nullum est corruptibile, quod non corrumpetur, et quod nullum generabile, quod non generabitur. Ad quod probandum talem adducit rationem: quia aliter non esset impossibile contradictoria simul verificari. Nam possibile posito in esse nullum sequitur impossibile. Quod ergo possibile est generari, pono quod generabitur. Tunc arguitur sic: possibile generari non generabitur, sicut conceditur ab adversario. Sed illud possibile generari generabitur per positionem possibilis in esse. Ergo sequitur quod hoc, quod generabitur, non generabitur, quod est de eodem contradictoria simul verificari.»

For this Aristotelian doctrine of modality and its medieval interpretations see S. *Knuuttila* (ed.), Reforging the Great Chain of Being, Studies of the History of Modal Theories, Dordrecht 1981, esp. 163—259.

and not-will (nolle) and as a result of its consideration defers its act (non velle), it follows that the act of willing, which the will was said to be capable of, is never realized. Consequently, something capable of generating will not generate, which implies a contradiction.[25] This argument, according to Buridan, has led many to believe that everything happens by necessity. »Contingency» would then only mean that the necessary alterations of agents cause different effects at different moments of time.[26] This view seems to have some support in the writings of Aristotle and Averroes.[27]

Buridan does not try to refute argument 7.3. in this connection. After giving his solution he returns, however, to the determinist arguments in order to criticize them. He maintains the distinction between natural and voluntary agents and argues for the activity of the voluntary agent. After doing that he goes on to discuss argument 7.3.

The same will is able to will or not-will, but it cannot do both simultaneously. Thus, if the proposition 'it is possible to will and not-will' is understood *de dicto,* P (p & ~p), it is false, but if it means *de re,* Pp & P~p, it is true. However, these two alternatives are compossible only as potencies.[28] The axiom »omnia generabile generabitur» can be treated in an analogous way. If we assume that something capable of

---

[25] 37 ra: »Hec ergo ratio Aristotelis et Commentatoris fiet ad propositum: si voluntas potest velle et nolle idem, ceteris eodem modo stantibus, et potest sic determinari ad non velle, ponamus ergo quod totaliter se determinet ad non velle. Tunc nunquam vellet, quod poterat velle, et ita actus volendi, cum sit generabilis, nunquam generabitur, quod etiam ratio predicta reprobat.»

[26] 37 ra—rb: »Propter quas rationes multi fuerunt coacti dicere quod omnia futura de necessitate evenirent sic quod omnis effectus novus ex aliarum preexistentia rerum necessitatur, ut quando evenit, eveniat, et quando non, non, et quod contingentia sunt solum attendenda ex hoc quod passiva principia sunt in potentia, ut in diversis temporibus diversos effectus recipiant secundum alterationes necessarias agentium.»

[27] 37 rb.

[28] 37 vb: »Ad aliam dicendum est quod utrumque est possibile ipsi voluntati, scilicet velle et nolle, sed tamen incompossibilia. Potest ergo voluntas in quodlibet seorsum ab altero exire, vel etiam quodlibet instanti seu qualibet hora, sed non potest exire in utrumque simul. Unde illa propositio: 'voluntas potest simul velle et nolle' est duplex. Nam si simul determinet ista duo verba: 'velle' et 'nolle', propositio est falsa. Sed si determinet ly potest, propositio est vera. Simul enim est in potentia, ut velit et ut nolit.»

generating never generates, then the proposition which says that the same thing will generate is false because of incompossibility.[29]

It can be seen that in this answer Buridan does not accept the Aristotelian axiom »omnia generabile generabitur». He admits, however, that if we assumed the world to be eternal, as the Philosopher did, the axiom would hold better. But even then generation and corruption would be inevitable only »loquendo de eo quod est generabile et corruptibile subiective intelligendo non de subiecto propinquo sed remoto» and »terminative loquendo secundum speciem licet non secundum individuum».[30] By using this terminology Buridan refers to his commentary *De caelo et mundo,* where he introduces these distinctions in Book I, quest. 23—25. There he argues that even in the natural course of things some possibilities are not actualized. Concerning the matter (subiective), all possible substances come into being but not all possible accidents. Concerning the form (terminative), all possible species actualize but not all possible individuals.[31] The supernatural possibilities are a special case; they are not examined in this question.[32]

To sum up, the first question of the third book refutes determinism and defines the extension of possible freedom. Freedom of opposition means that at a given instance there are more than one incompossible possible ways of acting. The will has a partial activity of its own in

[29] 37 vb: »Ad aliam per idem dicendum est quod: cum de aliquo corruptibili aut generabili positum fuerit quod nunquam generabitur vel nunquam corrumpetur, illa suppositione stante propositio dicens quod ipsum generabitur vel ipsum corrumpetur, est propositio falsa. Quoniam licet ipsa non sit secundum se impossibilis, tamen ipsa est alteri illi incompossibilis.»

[30] 37 vb: »Concedo tamen quod: si materia esset perpetua, sicut ponit Aristoteles primo Celi et Mundi, rationes Aristotelis ibidem si convenienter exponantur, necessario concluderent, quantum esset ex communi cursu nature, quod omne corruptibile materiale corrumpetur et omne generabile materiale generabitur, loquendo de eo, quod est generabile et corruptibile, subiective, intelligendo non de subiecto propinquo sed remoto. Similiter hoc esset dicto modo necessarium de eo, quod esset generabile et corruptibile, terminative loquendo secundum speciem, licet non secundum individuum.»

[31] Cf. *Iohannis Buridani* Quaestiones super libris Quattuor De caelo et mundo, ed. E.A. Moody, Ann Arbor 1942, 114—124.

[32] 37 vb: »Utrum autem supernaturaliter corruptibile potest perpetuari virtute liberi agentis: nec ille rationes Aristotelis dicunt nec contradicunt.» — On the supernatural possibilities cf. also Buridan's commentary De caelo et mundo, Book I, quaest. 23—25.

choosing between those possibilities. This view of Buridan's could be characterized Scotistic or Ockhamistic rather than traditionally Aristotelian, because he argues that free will has some activity of its own and that the axiom »omnia generabile generabitur» is not valid. It should be noticed, however, that he does this in order to refute determinism and to define the extension of possible human freedom and concludes only that this extension is not limited by the Aristotelian axioms discussed above. He does not consider yet the interrelation of will and intellect in action. Buridan's refutation of determinism implies only that the voluntary agent can have more than one genuine possible choice when considering its action. The freedom of opposition does not imply that the will is the primary instance which chooses between opposites. On the contrary, the will only has partial activity, and this activity consists mainly of the will's freedom to defer its act. In the following questions III 2—5 Buridan studies more closely this basic doctrine of his psychology and action theory. Before we can proceed to his treatment of moral weakness, we must also take a closer look on his view of human psychology.

The second question of the third book deals with the activity of the will in the case of freedom of opposition.[33] In order to perform an action the soul must, according to Buridan, receive information which is necessary for the acts of intellect and will. The reception of the intelligible content of an object always precedes the other activities of the soul. After receiving this information the soul can perform an act of intellection, which in turn leads to further consideration. The act of volition can take place only after the intellectual consideration has lead to a judgement. The soul is called a passive will insofar as the reception is concerned, whereas the active will refers to the production of the act of volition.[34]

---

[33] 37 vb: »Utrum voluntas sit activa illorum actuum oppositorum, in quorum utrumque ipsa potest libere, ceteris eodemmodo se habentibus iuxta determinata in alia questione?»

[34] 41 ra—rb: »Potest ergo dici quod ipsa anima est activa et receptiva omnis intellectionis et omnis volitionis, sed forte quod hoc non est totaliter secundum idem. Imo substantia gravis secundum seipsam est in potentia ad movere deorsum, et potest agere illum motum, secundum quem informat actum gravitatis; ita anima secundum seipsam potest intellectionem vel volitionem recipere, sed agere eam non potest, nisi secundum quod aliquo priori actu informata. ... Videtur ergo michi quod anima, informata ipse intelligibili ab obiecto, potest in se formare actum intelligendi, et ipsa simplicibus intellectionibus informata potest in se formare actum ponendi et postea

120

An intelligible object is needed in order that the act of intellection may be produced. The intellection is a necessary prerequisite for all further consideration and acting.[35]

In questions 3—5 this process of consideration and its relation to the will is analyzed closer. In the third question it is asked »whether the act of volition or nolition is preceded in the will by some other act or any other mediating disposition through which the act of volition comes into being in the same will».[36] According to Buridan, the ethical judgement of the practical intellect generates an act of complacence or displacence in the will. This act is followed by the act of acceptation or refutation, which is an actual inclination of the will and leads immediately to action if no external hindrance is present. If the action under consideration leads to results which are at the same time both positive and negative, the will receives the acts of complacence and displacence simultaneously.[37]

---

actum dividendi, saltem quo ad principia per se nota et postea actum discurrendi et sic consequenter. Et ita, quantum ad actum volendi, dicam: quod ipsa anima informata aliquo actu priori, puta vel iudicio de bonitate aut malitia volibilis vel quadam complacentia vel displicentia sicut dicetur post, potest se movere ad actum volendi. Sicut ergo eadem res, scilicet anima, dicitur voluntas passiva secundum quod potest actum volendi recipere et dicitur voluntas activa secundum quod potest actum ipsum producere. Hoc autem est secundum quod informata est actu priori predicto.»

[35] 41 va: »In substantia enim anime nostre non est sufficiens activum et sufficiens passivum intellectionis et volitionis, cum ad primos actus requiratur obiectum, et ad posteriores actus requirantur actus primi necessario. Nam obiecta necessario requisita ad actus primos et primi necessarii ad posteriores habent se ad actus illos, quibus sunt necessarii, vel passive vel active, aut principaliter aut dispositive.»

[36] 41 va: »Utrum actum volendi aut nolendi precedat in ipsa voluntate aliquis alter actus aut alia quecumque dispositio, mediante qua actus volendi fiat in ipsa voluntate?»

[37] 42 rb: »Ita iudicium, vel anima informata iudicio de bonitate vel malitia obiecti, primo generat in ipsa voluntate complacentiam quandam in obiecto vel displicentiam in obiecto, mediantibus quibus ipsa voluntas acceptare potest obiectum vel refutare, quae quidem acceptatio vel refutatio sunt iam actuales inclinationes voluntatis, ad quas motus consequitur, si non fuerit impedimentum, post quem motum voluntas figitur et quiescit in bono adepto, quae quidem quies vel fixio, dicitur delectatio, vel si fuerit impedimentum a prosecutione boni vel fuga mali, fiet in ipsa voluntate tristitia. Modo ergo diceretur quod: si obiectum fuerit voluntati presentatum sub ratione boni, tunc statim causabitur necessario in ipsa voluntake dictus actus complacentie. Et si fuerit sibi presentatum sub ratione mali, causabitur actus displicentie. Et si presentetur simul sub ratione bone et mali, causabuntur in ea simul utrique actus, scilicet complacentia ex obiecto illo et displicentia.»

The first act of the will (complacence/displacence) differs from the second act in two respects: whereas complacence and displacence are compossible and do not immediately lead to action, the acts of acceptation and refutation are incompossible and are followed by action. The freedom of the will pertains to its second act: the will can either accept or refute the proposed action or it can defer its act.[38] On the contrary, the will does not have any freedom in its first act, because the first act is only a passive reception of the intellectual judgement. Freedom is ascribed to the second act. This is also shown by the fact that merit and sin do not refer to complacence and displacence but to the actual acceptations and refutations performed by voluntary agents.[39] Moreover, Buridan illustrates the difference between the two acts of volition by pointing out that the proper act of volition is the second act of the will, not the first.[40]

For Buridan the possibility of deferring the act of volition is of special importance. The freedom of not being compelled to choose immediately between acceptation and refutation is very useful in practical life, says

[38] 42 rb—va: »Complacentia enim et displicentia circa idem opus non opponuntur, si fuerint secundum diversas rationes in tempore illo compossibiles in eodem. Sed quia acceptatio et refutatio sunt impetus ad actum prosequendum vel fugiendum, et isti motus, scilicet prosecutio vel fuga, propter contrarietatem sunt incompossibiles in eodem, ideo etiam non possunt simul in voluntate fieri huiusmodi acceptatio vel refutatio, sed voluntas libere potest acceptare opus ilud sine refutatione, vel refutare sine acceptatione, vel etiam nec refutare nec acceptare, sed differre, ut videtur michi quod quasi quilibet homo experiri potest in seipso.«

[39] 43 ra: »Cum igitur dictum fuerit primo quod voluntas non est activa sui primi actus sed passiva tamen, et quod libertas non est conveniens passivo in quantum passivum est, sed potius activo in quantum activum, non videtur inconveniens concedere quod voluntas non sit libera sive domina sui primi actus. Ita secundum quod, ceteris omnibus eodem modo se habentibus sive existentibus, ipsa possit in ipsum et ipsius oppositum, sed ipsa libere est domina sue acceptationis aut refutationis consequentis. Et hoc sufficere videtur videlicet quod voluntas sit illorum actuum domina, in quibus ex isti meritum vel peccatum; modo videtur quod in complacentia vel displicentia predictis nec mereamur nec peccemus, sed in obiecti totius acceptatione aut refutatione.«

[40] 43 ra—rb: »Mihi videtur, dicendum quantum ad primum articulum iam allegatum, quod actus simplicis complacentie vel displicentie non est actus volendi aut nolendi proprie, sed nolle aut velle acceptare et refutare. Nam si petatur a continente viro: 'vis tu cognoscere talem mulierum', non respondebit: 'volo'. Sed dicet: 'vellem, si non esset inhonestum vel peccatum'.«

Buridan, because a further consideration often reveals new aspects which affect the will's decision.[41] However, the deferment of the volition should not be the final decision.[42] The fourth and fifth question analyze how this possibility of deferring the volition for further consideration functions in the process of decision-making.

The fourth question asks whether it is possible for the will to will the lesser good instead of the greater good.[43] The same problem as asked in a more generalized form in the fifth question: »Whether it is possible for the will to will something against or in addition to the judgement of the reason?»[44] Buridan makes three conclusions: firstly, the will can defer its act even if the intellect has judged it good to will the object concerned. The will does this in order that the intellect may inquire further of the alternatives.[45] Secondly, it is not possible for the will to will something that the intellect hasn't judged to be good in some way or another.[46] Thirdly, the will can will against part of the intellectual judge-

---

[41] 42 va: »Ad cuius evidentiam est sciendum quod libertas, secundum quam voluntas potest non acceptare quod sibi presentatum fuerit sub ratione boni vel non refutare quod presentatum est sub ratione mali, prodest valde nobis ad vite directionem pro tanto, quia in multis, in quibus prima facie sunt alique rationes bonitatis apparentes, latent sepe mille malicie, vel annexe vel consequentes, propter quod acceptare illud quod apparebat bonum esset nobis inconveniens et damnosum. Et sic etiam, quod prima facie videtur esse malum, habet aliquando bonitatem latentem propter quam refutasse illud esset nobis malum.»

[42] 42 va—vb: »Sed tamen illa potestas non accipiendi vel non refutandi non prodest nobis finaliter, ut in huiusmodi non acceptatione vel non refutatione sistamus. Hoc enim esset impedimentum ad opus nobis debitum auferre. Sed illa potestas nobis prodest, ut ante obiecti acceptationem vel refutationem inquiramus de omni bonitate vel malicia, qui illud obiectum consequitur, vel ei annectitur.»

[43] 43 rb: »Utrum propositis duobus bonis per rationem, maiori bono et minori bono, incompossibilibus, voluntas dimisso maiori bono possit velle minus bonum?»

[44] 44 rb: »Utrum voluntas possit velle contra vel praeter iudicium rationis?»

[45] 44 vb: »Prima est quod voluntas potest illud non velle, quod per intellectum iudicatum esse bonum. Aliter enim non esset domina sui actus. Dictum enim fuit prius quod voluntas potest differre actum volendi, ut antea fiat inquisitio, si bonitati apparenti fuerit aliqua malicia consequens vel annexa. Potest etiam illud non velle propter annexam tristiciam vel laborem. Et eodemmodo dicendum est quod voluntas potest non nolle, quod intellectus iudicat esse malum.»

[46] 44 vb: »Secunda conclusio est quod voluntas non potest velle illud, in quo intellectui nulla apparet bonitatis ratio, quoniam tale nullomodo esset presentatum intellectui seu voluntati sub ratione volibilis. Et eodemmodo dicendum est quod voluntas non potest nolle, licet possit non velle, illud, in quo nulla apparet intellectui

ment, although not totally against it. The third conclusion is related to cases in which the action under consideration has both positive and negative implications. The will can, for example, either will to commit adultery if it chooses pleasure or refute to will it if it chooses chastity.[47]

In these three conclusions Buridan sums up his conception of the interaction of will and intellect. The freedom of the will pertains to its second and proper act, which can be acceptation, refutation or deferment. In order to will something this way the will always needs the judgement of intellect, which generates in the will an act of complacence (if presented sub ratione boni) or displacence (if presented sub ratione mali) or both. Even in the case of deferment this first act is needed: the intellect must in its judgement come to the conclusion that further consideration may be needed. Buridan seems to think, however, that further consideration always appears sub ratione boni if the intellectual judgement generates both the act of complacence and the act of displacence in the will.[48] In all such cases the will is free to defer its act; moreover, according to the first conclusion the will can always defer its act in order to investigate the possible hidden consequences. This doctrine seems to imply that most, if not all, human choices are somehow ambiguous and uncertain. The first conclusion even implies that in order to be »domina sui actus» the will has to have the possibility of doubting all reasons presented by the intellect. Still another case is when the intellect has determined the end aimed at but does not yet fully comprehend the means which lead to the desired end. By deferring its act the will moves the intellect to consider further the means.[49]

ratio malicie, quia tale nullomodo est presentatum intellectui sub ratione fugibilis vel refutabilis.»

[47] 44 vb: »Tercia conclusio est quod voluntas potest velle illud, quod aliquo modo iudicatum est esse malum, et nolle illud, quod aliquo modo iudicatum est esse bonum. Sicut si adulterium apparuerit inhonestum et delectabile, voluntas non obstante inhonestate potest velle adulterium ratione delectationis vel potest non velle ratione inhonestatis. Et ita est de illo, qui tempore tempestatis proicit merces in mare. Et hec dicta satis fuerunt prius. Sic igitur patet quod voluntas potest velle contra partem iudicii, sed non contra totum vel preter totum.»

[48] 44 vb: »Similiter etiam dico quod voluntas nunquam movet intellectum ad consiliandum, nisi intellectus preiudicaverit quod considerare illud obiectum est bonum. Nec est inconveniens quod intellectus actus cognoscat aliquod obiectum sub una ratione et dubitet de eo sub alia, et quod tunc iudicet bonum esse considerare ulterius circa ipsum.»

[49] 44 va—vb: »Solutio: dicendum est quod ipsa voluntas movet intellectum ad

In his treatment of the interrelation of will and intellect John Buridan stresses the role of intellect: although the will can act against part of the intellectual judgement, it must finally choose one of the alternatives presented sub ratione boni by the intellect. Buridan is, however, far from being intellectualist in the Thomistic sense. Although the will's freedom of choice is restricted to ambiguous cases, i.e. either when a deferment of volition is needed or when both alternatives are presented sub ratione boni, the extension of this freedom seems to be very large in practical life. According to Buridan the will can defer its act whenever it wishes further consideration. This possibility implies that the will plays a very active role in practical decision-making, because rational inquiry often shows that all alternatives have some ratio bonitatis, which gives the will the possibility of accepting or refuting the object according to this ratio.

Our conclusion thus means that Buridan sees the human choice as an ambiguous and often uncertain process. On the basis of this result we could formulate the hypothesis that it is the central role of uncertainty in the process of decision-making and action which distinguishes Buridan's action theory both from the Aristotelian and the voluntaristic traditions. During the following analysis of moral weakness it shall also be our task to examine this hypothesis somewhat closer.

III

John Buridan discusses moral weakness in questions 3—17 of Book VII. We shall restrict our analysis to questions 3, 5, 6, 7 and 8, which are of special interest for Buridan's action theory. Buridan is well aware of the various connotations which the term 'continence' has received during the centuries and distinguishes between the following equivocal meanings: 1) refraining from sexual intercourse, 2) temperance, 3) a sub-species of temperance and 4) a habit which resists passions but does not extinguish

---

considerandum, ut inveniat medium valens ad attingendum finem volitum. Hoc autem non posset esse, nisi per intellectum sibi presentatum sub ratione boni hoc, quod est consiliari ad talem medium inveniendum. Sicut igitur hoc iudicat intellectus esse bonum, ita hoc vult voluntas. Unde sicut intellectus non cognoscit determinate hoc medium quod postmodum invenit, ita nec voluntas determinate fertur in illud medium, sed fertur in consiliatum ad inveniendum medium. Et hoc cognoscit intellectus et iudicat esse bonum. Cum autem intellectus hoc determinatum medium invenerit et iudicaverit esse bonum, tunc voluntas poterit determinate velle ipsum et non ante.»

them. He stresses that in his treatment of continence and incontinence the term is used in the fourth, Aristotelian sense.[50]

The third question of Book VII asks whether continence is located in the will or in the sensitive appetite.[51] During the treatment of the problem it becomes obvious that continence and incontinence should be located in such a potency of the soul where it is possible to be determined in more than one way (aliter et aliter se habere) in order that both qualities, continence and incontinence, could be realized. It is argued that neither the intellect nor the sensitive appetite can change their judgement; therefore it must be the will where those qualities are located.[52] In spite of this argument Buridan prefers the view that continence and incontinence cannot be primarily located in the will, because the will must follow the intellect. Weakness of the will is therefore due to the weakness of the intellect. This view will be better illustrated later.[53]

In his solution Buridan asserts, however, that continence and incontinence can also be located both in the sensitive appetite and in the will, because all potencies of the soul are affected by the reasons given for and against the proposed action.[54] More interesting than this sol-

[50] 141 vb — 142 ra: »Dicendum est breviter quod phylosophi sepe utuntur equivoce nomine continentie. Sepe enim continentia capitur pro omni abstinentia ab actibus venereis. Et est sic idem quod virginitas vel vidualis castitas, de quibus in tertio libro satis dictum fuit. Aliquando autem capiuntur universaliter pro temperantia, ita quod continentia et temperantia sunt nomina sinonima et ita capit eam Seneca. Et sic continentia dicitur virtus sicut temperantia. Alio etiam modo capitur pro specie seu parte quadam temperantie, et ita videtur loqui Tullius de ea. Aliomodo capitur pro habitu, quo insistentes rectitudini rationis resistimus passionibus in nobis vehementibus existentibus non auferentes totum tractum ipsarum, propter quod operi nostro complacentia quedam vel displicentia annexa est. Et istomodo determinat Aristoteles de ea in hoc libro, et sic etiam capio in presenti questione.«
[51] 141 ra: »Utrum continentia sit in voluntate subiective vel in appetitu sensitivo?«
[52] 141 ra—rb.
[53] 141 rb: »Tamen adhuc est dubitatio contra istos, quia sicut in adventu passionis voluntas cadit ab electione recta, ita et ratio tunc infirmatus. Imo cum actus voluntatis sit posterior naturaliter actus intellectus, videtur quod infirmitas voluntatis eveniat propter infirmitatem rationis. Imo forte dicitur nomina continentie et incontinentie non esse primo ex parte voluntatis, sed prius ex parte rationis. De his autem magis videbitus infra.«
[54] 141 rb: »Ego puto esse dicendum de continentia et incontinentia sicut in fine primi libri dictum fuit de virtute et malicia. Videlicet quod in appetitu sensitivo potest

ution is its consequence that continence and incontinence occur in situations where a double inclination (duplex inclinatio) exists. In a such situation the will has reasons both to follow and to avert, to accept and to refute the proposed alternative, but neither of the reasons is compelling or complete.[55] In other words, both accepting and refuting passion are presented somehow *sub ratione boni*. This situation of double inclination in which the incontinent person acts is in many respects similar to the model of rational volition presented in Book III. In the following questions these similarities are explicated further.

When considering the next problem »Whether continence could be called a virtue»[56] Buridan asserts that both reasons which cause the double inclination, ratio delectationis and ratio turpitudinis, are formed in the sensitive appetite.[57] This is due to the fact that the sensitive appetite innately both follows pleasure and obeys reason. The person concerned follows the stronger inclination of the two.[58] Because the continent per-

---

poni continentia quidam et incontinentia, et quod etiam in voluntate ponenda est continentia et incontinentia; et quod illa, quae est in voluntate, principalior est ea, quae ponitur in appetitu sensitivo. Nam in quacumque potentia potest esse simul circa idem obiectum inclinatio ad prosequendum ratione delectationis sensualis, et inclinatio ad fugiendum ratione turpitudinis iudicate per rationem, vel etiam econtra. Ubi circa idem obiectum invenitur simul inclinatio ad fugiendum propter sensuaiem tristitiam et inclinatio ad prosequendum propter decentiam ratione iudicatam, ibi potest poni continentia et incontinentia. Sed dicte inclinationes simul inveniri possunt in appetitu sensitivo et in voluntate, igitur etc. Maior videtur manifesta, quoniam si in illa potentia vincat inclinatio ad passionem illam, quae est ad rationem, erit incontinentia, et si econverso, erit continentia. Minor satis apparere possit ex dictis in ultimis questionibus primi libri et ex dictis in tertio libro capitulo de voluntario et involuntario.»

[55] Cf. the previous note and 141 va: »Et mercator in mare tempestate veniente inclinatur ad salvandum merces propter lucrum, et ad perdendum eas propter sanitatem sui corporis. Et universaliter: ubicumque iudicatum fuerit in eodem esse rationem aliquam bonitatis et rationem aliquam malicie, potentia nata sequi illa iudicia poterit habere duplicem inclinationem, Hanc quidem ad prosequendum, illa autem ad fugiendum, quamvis ille non sint efficaces et complete.»

[56] 141 vb: »Utrum continentia debeat dici virtus?»

[57] 142 rb: »Nam continens simul trahitur ad prosequendum idem ratione delectationis apparentis et ad fugiendum ratione turpitudinis. Et non intelligo quod unus tractus sit in appetitu sensitivo solum et alter in voluntate solum, sed in utroque appetitu puto hunc duplicem esse tractum.»

[58] 142 rb: »Appetitus enim sensibilis est innatus sequi delectabile et est innatus obedire rationi. Propter quod secundum diversas rationes potest simul ad utramque partem inclinari. Et cum appetitus sensitivus organica virtus existens videatur immediate

127

son also has some complacence towards doing wrong, continence is only an incomplete virtue; accordingly incontinence is only an incomplete malice.[59] It should be noticed that with this conclusion Buridan does not want to object to the Parisian condemnation of 1277, which condemned the sentence »Quod continentia non esset essentialiter virtus».[60] Buridan repeatedly underlines his accordance with the Parisian condemnation; it is this question where he distinguishes between the equivocal menings of continence and says that his inquiry pertains to the Aristotelian conception of continence, which presupposes that the opposing complacence or displacence is not extinguished.[61]

The sixth question asks whether it is possible to possess simultaneously contrary judgements concerning the action to be realized.[62] The argument *quod sic* maintains that continence and incontinence would not otherwise be possible. The incontinent person has a double inclination, and he is conscious of both inclinations, as we can see in the case of penitents who confess that they knew they were doing wrong but could not refrain.[63] It is easiest to outline Buridan's complex answer if we

movere membra ad operandum, videtur quod ad illud operandum moveat ea, ad quid fortius inclinatur. Immo puto, si continens operatur secundum rationem, quod appetitus eius plus habeat de inclinatione ad obediendum rationi quam ad sequendum passionem. Et ita videtur magis bonus quam malus.»

[59] 142 rb: »Consummata videtur ergo quod continentia non sit virtus proprie accepta nec appetitus sensitivi in appetitu sensitivo nec voluntatis in voluntate. Sed quod sit habitus, adhuc incompletus, sicut tepiditas non caliditas in summo, sed est caliditas incompleta. Et sic etiam incontinentia non est completa malicia, sed est propinqua sibi, propter quod ipsa est vituperabilis.»

[60] The theses condemned by bishop Stephan Tempier can be found in *R. Hissette,* Enquête sur les 219 articles condamnés à Paris le 7 Mars 1277, Philosophes Médiévaux Tome XXII, Louvain-Paris 1977. For this sentence cf. *Hissette* op.cit., 297—298; *M. Grabmann,* Gesammelte Akademieabhandlungen, Paderborn 1979, 618 and *Thomas Aquinas,* Summa Theologiae II/II, q 155 ar 1.

[61] 141 vb — 142 ra (cf. footnote 50).

[62] 142 va: »Utrum de aliquo operabili possint haberi simul contraria iudicia?»

[63] 142 va: »Arguitur quod sic, quia aliter non possumus simul circa idem habere contrarias inclinationes, scilicet unam ad prosequendum et aliam ad fugiendum, cum appetitus non feratur in incognitum. Sed consequens est falsum, ut apparet in continentibus et in incontinentibus. Unde primo huius. Ad contraria enim motus incontinentum. Item incontinens, cum agit, appetit agere illud, quod agit. Et appetitus non fertur nisi in apparens bonum. Ergo apparet sibi quod bene agit. Et tamen sepe confitetur se scire quod non bene agit. Dicit enim aliquando reprehendentibus ipsum: 'scio quod non bene ago, sed non possum abstinere'.»

begin from his final answer to this argument. The two inclinations of the incontinent person are not, so Buridan says, both actual simultaneously. *Extra passionem* the incontinent refrains from doing wrong but *in passione* he commits sin. It can be said that the intellect can produce simultaneously both the reason for complacence and the reason for displacence, because they are not incompossible. But where the acceptation or refutation is concerned the intellect must give the single and final judgement. In the case of double inclination this judgement is weak (iudicium debilis); accordingly, the acceptation is weak (acceptatio debilis) and the will is confused (voluntarium mixtum).[64]

Buridan thus refutes the argument *quod sic* by using his previous model of twofold volition. The two opposite first acts of the will incline the will to perform its second and proper act in two incompossible ways. The two inclinations are actualized successively in the case of an incontinent person: after committing sin he suffers regret. He does not simultaneously possess contrary judgements concerning the second and proper act of the will although he has both complacence and displacence towards it. As a result of this situation his judgement is »weak» and »confused».

Before reaching this solution Buridan distinguishes between four different grades of how the intellect can estimate the truth of its judgement: 1. There is no evidence for or against the truth of the judgement. An example of this case is the question whether the total number of stars is even. 2. There is probable but not decisive evidence for both alternatives. 3. There is evidence for both sides but one side is more convincing. 4. The intellect is totally determined by one alternative.[65] In the

---

[64] 143 va: »Ad primam ergo rationem dici potest quod ad contraria sunt motus incontinentium sic quod appetitus extra passionem inclinatur ad fugiendum et in passione ad prosequendum et ita non simul. Vel etiam dicendum est quod intellectus simul iudicat idem esse delectabile et turpe; appetitus autem ob hoc statim innatus est habere circa illud complacentiam ratione delectationis et displicentiam ratione turpitudinis. Isto enim modo complacentia et displicentia non sunt opposite. Sed sicut intellectus non potest simul iudicare quod illud totum sit prosequendum et fugiendum, ita nec appetitus potest simul illud totum acceptare et refutare. Et sicut intellectus poterit iudicare totum esse prosequendum ratione delectationis, iudicio tamen debili et formidabili seu formidinali propter apparentem turpitudinem, ita appetitus poterit totum acceptare, sed tamen acceptatione debili et cum annexa displicentia propter turpitudinem; et erit voluntarium mixtum.»

[65] 143 ra: »Sed oportebit videre quod intellectus noster habens in se formatam

judgement of the fourth (the strongest) grade no other reasons can have power over the intellect. This kind of judgement is called »complete», whereas the other judgements are called »weak». In the case of a weak judgement the opposite reason remains effective in some way so that the judgement might change or it needs further evidence in order to be confirmed.[66]

Only in the case of weak judgement it is possible to maintain that contrary judgements exist simultaneously; therefore Buridan examines this alternative more closely. He presents two opposite views: some claim that contrary judgements are not substantially mixed, but exist as two separate possible alternatives of which only one can be actualized at one moment. With the weak judgement a slightest change can have the effect that the judgement is replaced by a view contrary to it. However, they cannot both exist simultaneously. Others maintain that there is no need to distinguish between judgements and their outward appearances, because contrary judgments are mixed with one another in a way which is manifested in the outward behaviour. According to this view, the end result of the practical reason in the case of contrary judgements lies between the opposites in a similar way as a warm temperature lies between hot and cold. A weak judgment would thus be a sort of compromise

---

propositionem, potest and iudicium de veritate ipsius se habere quadrupliciter: Unomodo quod ratione vel apparentia careat ad utramque partem, sicut forte esset de probleumate, an astra sint paria. Aliomodo quod habeat ad utramque partem rationes probabiles, sed tamen nondum determinantes ipsum ad unam partem vel ad aliam, sicut esset forte de probleumate, an forme substantiales elementorum maneant substantialiter in mixto. Tertiomodo quod per rationes ex una parte vincentes determinetur ad iudicium unius partis, sed tamen non sine formidine ad oppositum. Et iste intellectus est sicut vapor conversus iam in nubem, qui, licet sit magis agua quam aer, tamen multam habet dispositionem et tendentiam ad aerem. Quartomodo quod intellectus ex toto sit ad unam partem determinatus omni formidine remota et iste est sicut vapor cum perfecte factus sit aqua sic quod nulla remaneat in eo dipositio contraria aque.»

[66] 143 ra: »Dicam ergo quod sicut in aqua complete generata remote sunt omnes contrarie dispositiones, ita in completo iudicio de veritate partis omnes ablate sunt apparentie ad partem oppositam sic quod nullam habent vim super intellectum. Sed sicut nubes, licet verius sit aqua quam aer, tamen aliquam reservat aeris apparentiam et virtutem, ita in debile iudicio salvatur effectus apparentie partis opposite, reddens iudicium debile et faciliter in oppositum mutabile, vel adhuc et ad ampliorem determinationem.»

130

between the opposites. In this second way the both opposites could exist simultaneously.[67]

Buridan refutes the second view. Appearances are not identical with the judgements; this is shown by the fact that the apparent reasons do not lead to the final judgement immediately, because the act of the will can be deferred. A wise man examines all ambiguous cases thoroughly before making his decision.[68] Buridan makes two conclusions which show that in the case of weak judgement contrary judgements cannot exist simultaneously. Firstly, because the soul exists indivisibly throughout the body, the different senses cannot form contrary judgements at the same moment. Secondly, the *sensus communis* controls all judgements made by the external senses so that one judgement extinguishes all others that are contrary to it.[69]

---

[67] 143 ra: »Dici potest quod sicut aliqui ponunt formas aque et aeris non miscentur simul substantialiter, sed dispositiones ipsarum, ita aliqui ponunt quod iudicia contraria non miscentur simul substantialiter, sed dispositiones eorum, scilicet apparentie. Et isti habent dicere quod sicut materia non potest simul esse sub forma aque et aeris, tamen ipsa in nube existens sub forma aque propter dispositiones aeris convenientes transire potest faciliter in aerem, ita intellectus existens sub iudicio formidinali unius oppositi potest ex facili motivo transire in iudicium alterius oppositi. Alii autem ponunt quod non sit aliud iudicium quam apparentia, quod si concedatur, cum apparentie opposite (licet sub esse remisso) possit simul stare. Sic oporteret dicere quod et iudicia contraria, propter quod diceremus quod sicut tepidum in puncto non esset magis calidum quam frigidum vel econtra, propter quod neque simpliciter diceretur calidum neque frigidum, sic habens ad utramque partem apparentiam equalem, nec diceretur simpliciter iudicare unam partem nec aliam.«

[68] 143 rb: »Si queras, cui istarum viarum magis assentiam, dicam quod potest poni differentiam inter apperentiam et iudicium. Quoniam sepe, ut mihi videtur, expertus sum, quod cum rationes viderem ad utramque partem probabiles, tamen and neutram partem iudicii determinabam me, etiam neque novis rationibus ad unam partem vel ad aliam supervenientibus, sed in suspenso tenebam me. Et iterum videmus non omnes eque cito nec eque intense consentire apparentiis. Imo prudentis est prius examinare consilia. Apparentie namque videntur se tenere ex parte rerum et circumstantiarum suarum. Iudicium autem est actus ipsius intellectus circa apparentias.«

[69] 143 rb: »Prima ergo est quod, anima nostra indivisibilis existens in toto corpore et in qualibet parte eius, et iudicia, sicut dicit, non sunt solum in dispositionibus qualitativis vel quantitavis organorum subiective, sed in substantia anime. Propter quod, cum contraria non compatiantur se in eodem subiecto, impossible est hominem sive secundum unum sensum sive secundum diversos habere simul contraria iudicia. Alia causa assignatur, quia sensus exteriores habent ad sensum communem necessariam connexionem, ita quod statim iudicia eorum perveniunt ad ipsum. Ipse autem

As we have seen, the sixth question shows that incontinence is related to a so-called weak judgement, which is due to the object's being presented *sub ratione boni et mali.* Because the judgement is weak, the inclination of the will changes after the deviant action has been performed. It is interesting that Buridan denies the possibility of possessing contrary judgements simultaneously, because this solution implies that the incontinent person somehow does not realize he is doing wrong at the moment of deviant action. The next question is dedicated to this implication.

The seventh question asks »whether the incontinent man knows when he is doing wrong?»[70] Socrates, according to Aristotle, asserted that no one does wrong except through ignorance; the sin is therefore due to ignorance.[71] On the contrary, penitents often say that they knew they were doing wrong but could not abstain.[72] In his solution Buridan makes three distinctions: distinctions must be made between actual and habitual, universal and particular and, finally, between incomplete and perfect knowing.[73] On the basis of these distinctions he concludes that it is not possible to act against actual, particular and perfect knowledge, for it would presuppose the existence of simultaneous contrary judgements. However, if something remains ignored or incompletely considered or judged it is possible to act against this imperfect knowledge.[74]

---

idem existens non potest simul habere iudicia contraria. Iudicans autem unam partem extinguet iudicium partis opposite, sicut prius dicebatur.»

[70] 143 va.

[71] 143 va.

[72] 143 vb.

[73] 143 vb — 144 ra.

[74] 144 ra: »Et hec sit quarta conclusio, vel forte he due conclusiones ultime possent virtualiter poni sub tali distinctione. Scientiam actualem et particularem potest aliquis habere duplicem. *Unam* perfectam, ubi nichil remanet ignoratum nec inconsideratum nec iniudicatum pertinens ad operandum vel non operandum. Et tunc non est possibile agere contra scientiam, quia oporteret simul habere iudicia contraria. Nam si actu iudices non esse mechandum cum ista, et cum hoc actu iudices quod coire cum ea est mechari cum ea, oporteret te actu iudicare quod non est coeundum cum ea, quia, sicut apparet primo Posteriorum, inducens sub maiori minorem simul cognovit conclusionem. Hoc autem stante non coibis, nisi simul iudices coeundum et non coeundum esse. Et hec sit quinta conclusio. *Aliam* contingit esse scientiam particularem et actualem incompletam, ubi scilicet aliquid remanet ignoratum vel inconsideratum vel iniudicatum. Et tunc est possibile agere contra scientiam; non tamen contra directe et formaliter, sed sicut dicebatur in quarta conclusione. Et ista sit sexta conclusio.»

132

In these conclusions Buridan reasserts his view that incontinence is due to uncertainty caused by weakness of judgement. It can also be seen that Buridan's conception of incontinence differs significantly from the voluntaristic view of Walter Brugge and William of Ockham.[75] Although Buridan's doctrines of twofold volition, double inclination and weak judgement give the will a considerable amount of activity, he wants to preserve the primacy of intellect. In the case of perfect knowledge and complete judgement the will cannot act against the reason.

The last conclusions of the seventh question give a detailed description of the different phases of the incontinent action. Before and after passion the incontinent person can judge everything freely and rationally. Therefore penitence takes place after passion has ceased.[76] Because the incontinent person knows what is deviant before and after his action and as there is no forgetting there must be some habitual knowledge of doing wrong even during the action. Buridan admits that there is some universal and particular knowledge during the action.[77] This knowledge cannot, however, be actual, particular and perfect.[78] If, for example, an incontinent person confesses that he knew he was doing wrong with an actual, particular and perfect knowledge, he must be lying. If he tries to prove his knowledge by presenting some arguments during the passion, he does not really believe in them but just repeats the arguments as the drunk cites Empedocles in Aristotle's example.[79]

---

[75] Cf. the footnotes 10 and 11.

[76] 144 rb: »Dicam ergo quod incontinens, antequam in passione detentus sit et postquam a passione liberatus est, potest omnia libere attendere et cognoscere, et de omnibus absque ignorantia vel inconsideratione vere iudicare. Propter quod ipse scire potest scientia particulari actuali et perfecta, quoniam malum esset hoc agere, et quod male aget si hoc agat, et quod male egit si hoc egit, propter quod accidit ipsum penitentem esse, sicut dicit Aristoteles. Ergo post factum scit incontinens, quoniam male egit si hoc agat. Et ista sit septima conclusio.«

[77] 144 rb: »Octava conclusio est quod incontinens, dum incontinenter agit, scit in habitu, quoniam prave agit. Scivit enim ante et illud non est oblitus, quia cessante passione sciet idem, non de novo addiscens. Nona conclusio est quod incontinens, dum incontinenter agit, scit aliquomodo in actu, in universali vel etiam in particulari, non tamen directe vel non perfecta scientia, quoniam prave agit. Et hoc totum patet ex prioribus conclusionibus.«

[78] 144 rb: »Decima conclusio est quod nullus incontinens, dum incontinenter agit, scit, quoniam prave agit scientia actuali, particulari et perfecta, quod etiam totum manifestum est ex predictis.«

[79] 144 rb: »Si autem incontinens confiteatur se scire, quoniam male agit, scientia

After presenting these conclusions Buridan discusses their relation to the Parisian condemnation. Some doctors want to object to his conclusions by referring to two articles of the condemnation, namely: »Quod stante scientia in universali et in particulare in actu quod voluntas non possit in oppositum — error» and »Si ratio est recta quod necesse est voluntatem esse recta — error».[80] Buridan admits that a deviant will is likely to pervert the judgement of the intellect by prohibiting it taking into account any other reason than that delectation ought to be followed.[81] But to do wrong consciously is possible only if the knowledge is not perfect in the sense defined in the previous conclusions. It should be noticed that it is in accordance with the conclusions to say that one can sin against the conscience because one can act against actual knowledge.[82] In the same connection Buridan also answers some other accusations of intellectualism: If it is maintained that there would be no sin *ex certa malicia,* this is answered by the fact that a determined malignancy does not presuppose a true judgement but only a determined knowledge of the circumstances and a consciousness of doing wrong. If it is said that all sin would be caused by ignorance or that the will would not be free, one should consult the previous discussion in order to find the answer. Con-

---

actuali, particulari et completa, non confitetur verum. Et si aliquando rationem ad probandum quod male agit adducat vel repetat, tamen interiori mente non iudicat esse verum, quod dicit. Verbi gratia: si formet istum sillogismum: nullo casu mechandum est; sed nunc coire tecum est mechari; ergo non est nunc tecum coeundum, talis proponet maiorem propositionem, nichil tamen iudicans de ea, sicut ebrii vel maniaci proponunt verba Empedoclis, ut dicit Aristoteles. Et si isti, quando iudicent de maiori, tamen statim ad delectationem aspicientes cadunt ab illo iudicio.»

[80] 144 vb. Cf. *Hissette* 1977. 257—260.

[81] 144 vb: »Cum enim voluntas prava sit innata pervertere iudicium intellectus. Unde visum fuit in sexto quod malitia facit mentiri circa practica principia. Si ipsa sic inclinata fuerit ad delectabile prosequendum, quod ex ipsa delectabilis ostensione prosequatur ipsum, videtur quod ipsa, nisi seipsa ab huiusmodi inclinatione retinuerit, non permittit intellectum iudicare quod illud delectabile non sit prosequendum.»

[82] 144 rb—va: »Ad aliam concedendum est quod aliquis potest sciens agere male modis predictis et non aliter. Quando ergo dicitur quod nullum esset peccatum contra conscientiam, dicendum est quod ymo modis predictis potest enim aliquis agere id, quod actu scit esse inhonestum vel deo desplicere.»

For the sentence of Parisian Condemnation »Quod non est possibile esse peccatum in potentiis animae superioribus» cf. *Hissette* 1977, 261.

cerning the freedom of the will, Buridan underlines once again that the freedom means possibility to defer the volition.[83]

It should be noticed in this connection that Buridan's conception of incontinence could be criticized by his contemporaries for being too intellectualist. As we have seen, Buridan wants to preserve the primacy of the intellect but moderates it by introducing various new concepts which stress the uncertainty of human choice and give the will more or less the freedom to choose its reason in uncertain cases. This regulation of intellectualism differs remarkably from the Franciscan type of voluntarism which found its expression in the Parisian articles and later in Ockhamism.

The same discussion is continued under a slightly different aspect in the eighth question where it is asked whether the will necessarily follows the conclusion of practical intellect.[84] The arguments *quod non* point out that many instructions of the intellect are not followed by the will and that otherwise the will would not be free, as both Aristotle and the Parisian articles teach.[85]

Buridan's solution follows once again the line already sketched in previous questions. In order that the will follows the judgement the object must be judged good, not only universally but also for the person concerned.[86] Moreover, if the judgement is based only on a »partial» or »common» reason, i.e. it is not a total and specified judgement, the will is not compelled to an act of acceptation.[87] The most interesting part of

---

[83] 144 va: »Quando etiam dicitur quod nullum esset peccatum ex certa malitia, dicendum est quod peccatum ex certa malitia non dicitur, quia peccans, dum peccat, iudicet vere et cum certitudine se male agere, sed quia cum certitudine cognoscit omnes circumstantias operis sui, et cum hoc etiam cognoscit opus suum esse inhonestum et deo displicere, sicut statim dicebatur. Quando etiam dicitur quod omne peccatum esset ex ignorantia, dicendum est quod satis apparuit in prioribus libris, quomodo et quando debeat peccatum dici ex ignorantia. Quando etiam dicitur quod aliter non essemus domini actuum nostrorum et aliter voluntas non esset libera, dicendum est ex eo quod voluntas non dicitur libera, quia possit velle quod iudicatum est esse malum et hoc illo iudicio stante, sed quia ipsa stante iudicio de bonitate vel malitia potest differre actum volendi vel nolendi, sicut magis dictum fuit in tercio libro.»

[84] 144 vb: »Utrum voluntas necessario feratur in id, quod per rationem practicam conclusum est?»

[85] 144 vb — 145 ra. The sentence »Quod voluntas necessario prosequitur quod firmiter creditum est a ratione; et quod non potest abstinere ab eo quod ratio dictat» was also condemned in 1277. See *Hissette* 1977, 255—256.

[86] 145 ra.

[87] 145 rb: »Quarto dico quod, si quis iudicaverit aliquid esse sibi bonum secun-

the question are conclusions six and seven, in which Buridan introduces a distinction between dubious (dubium) and firm (certum) judgement. Even when the judgement of the intellect is free from deficiency (integre), the will is not compelled to follow it if the judgement is dubious. For example, if some action is entirely meritorious but it is dangerous to perform it, the will does not necessarily embrace it.[88] But if the judgement is firm the will follows it by necessity. A firm judgement should not be identified with a scientific, true judgement, because an opinion can also be called firm. Experience shows that the certainty of a judgement is not identical with its truth.[89]

This distinction is similar to the distinction between weak and complete judgement, but a dubious — firm distinction is theoretically more interesting, because it finally constitutes the criterion according to which the will must obey the intellect.

The seventh conclusion can be proved in the same way as the necessity of the act of complacence was proved in Book III, quest. 3 and further in the same way as it was shown that the greater good must always be

---

dum aliquam partialem rationem bonitatis solum, que scilicet in eodem compati possit aliquam rationem malicie, non est necesse voluntatem ferri illud secundum actum acceptationis, quoniam sua libertas de nichilo sibi deserviret. Et ista etiam conclusio satis declarata fuit in tercio libro. Quinto etiam dico quod, si quis iudicaverit aliquid esse sibi bonum secundum communem rationem bonitatis, dico: communem cogitare predicationis non est necesse voluntatem ferri in illud secundum actum acceptationis, quoniam iudicium secundum rationem communem est minoris efficacie quam iudicium secundum rationem specialem. Ipsa minus necessitabitur per iudicium commune.»

[88] 145 rb: »Sexto, si quis iudicaverit aliquid esse sibi bonum secundum rationem integre bonitatis, ita scilicet quod illud appareat bonum secundum omnem rationem bonitatis sic quod omnis ratio malicie excludatur, videtur michi, si iudicium fuerit dubium, quod nundum voluntas necessario acceptabit illud. Et credo quod hoc sit expertum. Aliqui enim confitentur se putare quod tale officium vel talis mercatura esset sibi honestum et delectabile et utile amicis suis et quod inde nullum malum consequeretur. Tamen propter dubium periculorum acceptare non audent.»

[89] 145 rb: »Septimo, si predictum iudicium fuerit certum omnino, videlicet quod homo credat firmiter sufficienter vidisse omnes circumstantias et combinasse et secundum earum combinationem credat firmiter illud esse sibi bonum secundum omnem rationem bonitatis et nullo modo malum, puto quod voluntas necessario acceptaret illud. Et non intelligo hic per certum iudicium idem quod iudicium verum vel scientificum, sed idem quod firmiter creditum omni exlusa formidine. Sic enim contingit opinionem veram vel etiam falsam esse certam.»

preferred. If the freedom of the will implies that we could choose the lesser good instead of the greater, freedom would not be a virtue but a vice, which is false. The freedom of the will means the possibility of deferring the volition for a while. The utility of this freedom is based on the fact that we are free in order to inquire into all possible consequences before the act of acceptance or refutation. Through this inquiry we can reach a perfect judgement which is firmly believed and does not include any doubts concerning the outcome of the action.[90]

Here we can see *expressis verbis* how the doctrine of uncertainty functions in Buridan's action theory. Freedom of the will is defined as the possibility of deferring the act of volition after the first, involuntary act of complacence and/or displacence. This freedom pertains to cases where a dubious judgement exists. If there were no dubious cases, no freedom would exist because a firm judgement of the intellect is necessarily followed by the action. The criterion for the will's obedience is the certainty of the intellectual judgement. The free will can help the intellect to form firmer judgements by temporarily deferring its volition. In dubious cases the will can freely choose its reason and, accordingly, the object presented, but in order to avoid errors in dubious cases it is better not to act immediately. Therefore a wise person always considers the alternatives thoroughly.

Buridan concludes the eighth question by reaffirming his opinion about the firm judgement.[91] There are some minor exceptions, as when

---

[90] 145 rb—va: »Illa etiam conclusio probatur sicut in tercia questione tercii libri probabatur quod in apparente bono voluntas necessario habeat complacentiam. Et sicut in quarta questione eiusdem libri probabatur quod voluntas dimisso maiori bono non possit acceptare minus bonum. Quoniam si stante dicto iudicio voluntas possit illud non acceptare, hoc sibi proveniret ex sua libertate, ut omnes concedunt. Sed consequens est falsum, quia tunc illa libertas esset mala conditio. Tota enim bonitas libertatis auferretur. Potestas enim non acceptandi bonum apparens vel non refutandi malum apparens non prodest nobis finaliter, ut in huiusmodi non acceptatione vel non refutatione sistamus, sed ut ante obiecti acceptationem vel refutationem inquiramus de omni bonitate vel malitia, que illud obiectum consequitur vel ei annectitur, ut tandem, quod est simpliciter melius, acceptemus et quod est simpliciter peius, refutemus. Ergo inquisitione facta plenarie sic quod iudicium sit perfecte creditum omni sublata formidine, nichil ultra prodest potestas non acceptandi sed obest, quia per ea possumus frustrari bono nostro etiam nobis manifeste ostenso.«

[91] 145 va: »Videtur michi, si quis iudicio certo certitudine prius exposita iudicaverit illud esse sibi bonum, non obstantibus maliciis apparentibus, quod voluntas

the goal aimed at is impossible or laborious to reach or when there is no necessary preference on either side; in such cases the will is free to approach both opposites even if the judgement is firm.[92]

IV

Our analysis has shown that John Buridan defends an original conception of the will's freedom in the third and seventh Book of his *Quaestiones super decem libros Ethicorum*. In Book III he refutes determinism and argues for the will's freedom; however, in Book VII he has to express many times his concordance with the Parisian Condemnation in order to avoid being accused for determinism and intellectualism. In spite of these two different positions Buridan's view is coherent and consistent.

It can be concluded that the analyzed questions deal with the problem of freedom under two different aspects: whereas the question 1 of Book III is interested in the existence of freedom of opposition, i.e. whether two incompossible alternatives can exist simultaneously, the other question is dedicated to various aspects of interrelation between will and intellect, which presuppose the existence of freedom of opposition.

In the first question of Book III Buridan defends a non-Aristotelian view of the will's freedom, which is based on the activity of the will and the refutation of the principle »omnia generabile generabitur». It was not the aim of this study to analyze these logical and metaphysical prerequisites of freedom any closer. In this connection it should be mentioned, however, that John Buridan is usually seen by modern scholars as a representative of »new» modal logic, which abandoned the Aristotelian so-called »statistical» interpretation of modality and found its expression in the John Duns Scotus's statement: »I do not call contingent that which is not necessary or not always, but that the opposite of which could have happened at the very same time it actually did.»[93] This in-

---

necessario acceptabit illud et hoc eisdem rationibus apparet cum conclusione precedente.»

[92] 145 va—vb.

[93] *J. Duns Scotus,* Tractatus de primo principio IV, 4; *S. Knuuttila,* 'Modal Logic', in: CHM, 342—357, especially 353, 355—357. See also Ria van der Lecq's Introduction in: *Johannes Buridanus,* Questiones longe super librum Perihermeneias, ed. Ria van der Lecq, Leiden 1983.

terpretation of modality is also a necessary prerequisite for the acceptance of Buridan's freedom of opposition.

The special interest of this paper was directed towards the problem of how Buridan understood the intellectualist Aristotelian action theory which causes philosophical problems in the treatment of moral weakness. Although Buridan's conception of freedom of opposition is non-Aristotelian, his view of human action was found to be so intellectualist that he had to defend himself in order to avoid being condemned as an Averroist by the Parisian articles of 1277.

The main result of this study was the conclusion that Buridan's view of incontinence and human action differs significantly both from voluntarism and intellectualism. This difference is primarily seen in his conception that uncertainty plays a central role in intellectual judgement. Only in the case of firm judgement (certum iudicium) is the will obliged to follow the intellect; otherwise the will is free either to choose its reason from the variety of all possible motives or to defer its act. In order to be firm the judgement need not be true but it must be actual, particular, complete and firmly believed so that there is not the slightest reason for not performing the action under consideration. If these conditions are not fulfilled the judgement is dubious (dubium) or weak (debile).

In the case of dubious judgement two contrary reasons always exist concerning the action to be performed. These contrary reasons necessarily cause the first potential inclinations in the will, namely the acts of complacence and displacence. The will is free to act its second and proper act according to either of these reasons if the judgement remains dubious. By deferring the act of volition and thus offering the intellect a chance for further consideration judgement can be examined and confirmed. For this reason it is often useful and wise to defer the act of volition in the case of a dubious judgement. The freedom of the will pertains to cases where a dubious judgement exists, because only then can a free will be of use and accordingly a virtue. In a firm judgement a free will would only cause harm by acting against the judgement or by deferring its act.

The habits of continence and incontinence are also related to a dubious judgement. Contrary reasons and the contrary first acts of the will cause a situation of double inclination (duplex inclinatio) in continent and incontinent persons. Whereas the continent person can follow a virtuous inclination, the will of an incontinent person follows the *ratio delectationis* and inclines towards it in its second act. But after the passion is extinguished, the other inclination comes into force and the incontinent person repents. The theological problem of penitence is thus related to incontinence; penitents have somehow possessed a double inclination and a dubious judgement.

This result shows that for Buridan the uncertainty is the central concept which explains both the free will and incontinence. If all judgements were firm neither free will nor incontinence would exist. Buridan's psychology is thus based on the primacy of intellect but he sees human action as a result of uncertain and ambiguous process in which the will is often free to choose its reason.

This explanation of incontinence differs from Aristotelism and Thomism as well as from Franciscan voluntarism. Neither of these traditions underline the role of uncertainty in connection with free will and incontinence. On the other hand, it is often argued that the late medieval and Renaissance period were characterized by a conviction that uncertainty and probabilism cannot be avoided in practical philosophy. It is not our task here to ask whether the philosophical standpoint of Buridanism had any influence in this development; we have only tried to show how the doctrine of uncertainty functions in Buridan's action theory. Let it be mentioned, however, that the discussion on probabilism and probabiliorism in Catholic moral theology during the 16th and 17th centuries, for example, reflects problems similar to the above analyzed questions of Buridan's commentary.[94]

---

[94] Cf. *T. Deman,* Probabilisme, Dictionnaire de theologie catholique 13, Paris 1936, 417—619; *Döllinger-Reusch,* Geschichte der Moralstreitigkeiten in der römisch-katholischen Kirche seit dem 16. Jahrhundert, Nördlichgen 1889, Neudruck München 1968, 1—96; *I. Kantola,* Omatunto subjektiivisena totuuteen pitäytymisenä, Thyrsus Gonzalezin esittämä ratkaisu moraalisen epävarmuuden ongelmaan probabilismikiistassa (Thyrsus Gonzalez on Moral Uncertainty), typewritten, Library of the Theological Faculty, Univ. of Helsinki; *S. Knuuttila,* Uuden ajan filosofisten ihmiskäsitysten uutuuksista (New Ideas in the Philosophical Anthropology of Modern Times), Ajatus 41, 139.

REIJO TYÖRINOJA

PROPRIETAS
VERBI

Luther's Conception of Philosophical and Theological Language
in the Disputation: Verbum caro factum est (Joh. 1: 14), 1539

INTRODUCTION: the Course of the Argument

In Luther's thought the question of the character of theological language is often in focus. In this respect especially some of his late disputations include interesting material. While criticizing the views of the others he also attempts to outline better alternatives. To what extent those proposed alternatives are dependent on the preceding theological and philosophical thought or to what extent they pose as real novelties, it is the question at issue.

In what follows I try to answer these questions by examining Luther's disputation *Verbum caro factum est* (1539). It deserves particular attention because the forty-two theses proposed by Luther and his responses to several counter-arguments seek to present a clearly argued whole.[1] His main interest is to define the relation between theology and philosophy in a way that is acceptable from the theological point of view. However, as we shall see, the term 'philosophy' in this disputation has for the most part a somewhat narrow definition. By 'philosophy' Luther means logic (dialectica), i.e. either syllogistic or terminist logic. I shall first describe the course of Luther's argument. Thereafter I shall try to exemplify some essential conceptual presuppositions which explain his views.

According to Luther, one must adhere to the principle that every truth is in agreement with every other truth (omne verum vero consonat). However, one must also acknowledge that what is true is not the same in diverse branches of learning (idem non est verum in diversis professionibus) (T1). In theology it is true that the word was made flesh, but in philosophy this is simply impossible and absurd. The predication »God is man» in philosophy is even more disparate than the predication »Man is an ass» (T2, 3). Therefore, it is erroneous to say that the same is true

---

[1] WA, 39 II, 1—33. See Appendix.

in philosophy and in theology (idem esse verum in philosophia et theologia) (T4). From the doctrine of predicables (ex predicabilium doctrina) it follows that God is man, therefore God is rational, sensitive animal, living, having a body, in fact is substance and a created being (T10). But Christians have to speak according to what has been prescribed and therefore such consequences (consequentiae) must simply be rejected (T11). In matters of faith there is no use of such subtle inventions as mediate and immediate suppositions (T12).

In philosophical reasonings theology clashes with the rules of philosophy but more often philosophy clashes with the rules of theology (T15). For instance, the following *syllogismus expositorius* is good (bonus): *Pater in divinis generat. Pater est essentia divina. Ergo essentia divina generat.* (T16) Likewise, the following *syllogismus communis: Omnis essentia divina est pater. Filius est essentia divina. Ergo filius est pater.* (T18) In both examples there are true premisses, but even so, the conclusion is false. Therefore contrary to the principles of philosophy from what is true follows what is false (ex vero sequitur falsum) and truth does not agree with truth (verum vero non consonat) (T17, 19).

This fact, however, is not caused by a defect in the syllogistic form, but by the unusual character of the matter which cannot be enclosed within the narrow confines of reason or syllogisms (rationis seu syllogismorum) (T20). This matter is not, however, contrary to logical truth, but it is outside, within, above, before, and beyond all logical truth (omnem veritatem dialecticam) (T21). In these syllogisms the form is the best one (forma optima), but as for the matter they are nothing (nihil ad materiam) (T26). In articles of faith one must have recourse to another dialectic and philosophy which is called the word of God and faith (T27).

One can see, according to Luther, that in regard to arts and sciences other than theology the same is not true in all of them (T29). For instance, it is false and an error to say that weights can be attached to a mathematical point or line. In the same manner it is false and an error in the genus of measurement to measure a pint with the measure of a foot or an ell (T30, 31). Something can be true in one area of philosophy, but false in another area of philosophy. When considering in this way particular arts one will never discover that the same is true in all of them. Much less can the same be true in philosophy and theology, because the difference between them is infinitely greater than that between the particular arts (T38, 39). For that reason it is more appropriate to keep logic or philosophy (dialectica seu philosophia) within its own sphere and learn to speak in new languages (loqui novis lingus) in the realm of faith outside of every sphere (extra omnem sphaeram) (T40).

Luther and the Double Truth Theory

In the preface of the disputation Luther says that he will argue against the theologians in Sorbonne in Paris who have determined that the same is true (idem esse verum) in theology as in philosophy and vice versa (7,10, A). When disputing the idea that those which are true in philosophy are also true in theology and vice versa (sint vera in theologia, quae in philosophia vera sunt et e contra), and arguing that the same cannot be true in the diverse branches of learning (7,24–26 A), Luther seems to commit himself to the some kind of double truth theory.

It is not quite clear to whom Luther in fact refers by those from Sorbonne who have »impiously condemned» those who have argued that the same is not true in philosophy and theology (T4, 5). The most important event of this kind was certainly the famous condemnation of 1277 when the Bishop of Paris, Etienne Tempier, condemned 219 propositions as errors and forbade the teaching of them. In this very year Pope John XXI (Petrus Hispanus who was elected the year before)[2] had asked the Bishop to investigate and report on the teaching in the faculty of arts in Paris. Instead of only reporting to the Holy See on the teaching in question Bishop Tempier called a commission of sixteen theologians (Henry of Ghent among them). As a result of the commission the teaching of 219 propositions was forbidden under penalty of excommunication.[3]

The condemned propositions covered different topics and were without any systematic order. In the background of the condemnation was the impact of the radical Aristotelian currents in philosophical and theological thinking. This more or less coherent body of philosophical and theological opinions has been usually called (since E. Renan) »Latin Averroism», or »heterodox Aristotelianism» (Van Steenberghen). The interpretation of Averroes, »the Commentator», upon Aristotle's philosophy

---

[2] See *De Rijk*, 1972, IX, XL.
[3] *Gilson*, 1985, 405—406.

was taken to be correct and authoritative in many respects.[4] This new form of Aristotelianism led to the producing of such views which theologians like Thomas Aquinas and Albert the Great, although supported by the Philosopher, had either rejected, or rendered so that a conflict with church doctrine was avoided. These issues were e.g. the limits of God's omnipotence, the eternity of the world, and the possibility of a soul (as a form of the body) surviving after death.[5]

In the prologue to the decretal Bishop Tempier condemns those who teaching errors under the influence of pagan writings say »that these things are true according to philosophy but not according to the Catholic faith, as if there were two contrary truths and as if the truth of Sacred Scripture were contradicted by the truth in the sayings of the accursed pagans.»[6] Whether anybody was a representative of a particular doctrine of double truth, is still suspect. From the viewpoint of the Aristotelian concept of science and metaphysics the very idea of double truth was inevitably absurd. Neither did the condemned propositions imply such an idea. Bishop Tempier's preface gives in fact an impression that it was an *ad hoc* attempt rather than a philosophical doctrine or systematically developed theory. Anyway, such a double truth theory cannot be found in Siger of Brabant or Boethius of Dacia, who were central figures in the controversy.

Siger of Brabant, for example, says that if certain premises are accepted then certain conclusions necessarily follow. But if those conclusions are contrary to the faith of the church, truth lies with the latter. Nevertheless, he would not maintain that the same thing could be simultaneously true and false.[7] Neither does Boethius of Dacia support the double truth theory. On the other hand, he firmly vindicates the independence of philosophy in its relation to theology, and a philosopher's

---

[4] See *Gilson,* 1985, 387—402, 406—410; *Maurer,* 1982, 192—207; *Copleston,* 1972, 199—212.

[5] The condemned 219 propositions have been translated in *Lerner & Mahdi,* 1963, 338—354. See for example propositions 13, 15, 17, 85, 115, 133, 178, 185, 189, 213, 219. (The translators' numbering is different from the original numbering.) On the impact of the condemnation on philosophy and theology, see *Grant,* 1982, 537—539, *Gilson,* 1985, 408—410, *Lohr,* 1982, 87—94.

[6] *Lerner & Mahdi,* 1963, 337.

[7] *Copleston,* 1972, 207. See also *Gilson,* 1985, 389—399; *Maurer,* 1982, 194—199.

right to pose questions and to answer them purely by rational reasons, even though these answers might clash with faith. Boethius thinks that a truly wise Christian keeps to both his faith and philosophy without attacking either one or the other. Both have their own place in the life of man. In fact this very attempt to determine the relation between philosophy and theology in the new way can be considered to be one of the distinctive marks of this so called »Averroism».[8]

In regard to Luther it is clear that he hardly felt any particular sympathy for those disputed pursuits as they were. One can see only a certain similarity in the desire to separate philosophy from theology. Considering Luther's argument, however, it is more essential to see, how he understands the statement of his opponents »esse idem verum in theologia et philosophia, et e contra» (7,10, A), and on the other hand, what he means when arguing against them »idem non sit verum in theologia et philosophia» (7,32–33, C), than to know at whom he is actually pointing.

In order to understand Luther's viewpoint we should outline those conceptual presuppositions by means of which his remarks and counterexamples actually function. For instance, we have to answer the question, what is the subject of »idem» in the phrase »idem non est verum in theologia et philosophia.» Is it the same thing (res), or is it the same proposition, which is true in one area but not in another, or is it something else?

First Luther makes a distinction between 'understanding' and 'believing' when he says »aliud esse intelligere, aliud credere». This fact makes the difference between theology and philosophy (7,26–28, A;33–34, C). Later in connexion with the seventh argument he makes a further distinction between 'thinking', 'understanding' and 'believing'. Man can think about many things (cogitare multa) which are beyond his capability to understand (extra captum), such as the word of God, all articles of faith, eternal life, etc. However, he can in no way believe in them (credi

---

[8] *Maurer,* 1982, 201—202. See *Gilson,* 1985, 399—402; *Copleston,* 1972, 204—206. Averroes himself attempted from the basis of Aristotle's philosophy to establish the independence of philosophical thinking. His admiration of Aristotle is well known. According to Averroes, »the doctrine of Aristotle is the supreme truth (summa veritas), because his intellect was the limit of the human intellect (finis humani intellectus). Therefore Aristotle can be regarded »as created and given to us by divine providence» so that »we might know all that can be known.» *Gilson,* 1985, 218—220.

nullo modo), because whether they are true (quod vera sint) or not, cannot be concluded from what they are themselves (concludere ex sese), for instance that which is infinite like God, can be made finite like man. If they could be understood they would also be believed (15,3–7, A).[9] Luther here wants to make a definite factual and conceptual difference between »thinking», »understanding» and »believing». Just as God created distinct spheres in heaven, so there are distinct spheres regarding these faculties (7,37–38, C). In the same way on earth every single thing and art (res et ars) has been put in its place and species, in which it ought to retain and not to turn aside from its centre (8,5–9, A).

Philosophy and theology also differ from each other because they have a different starting-point (primum) and aim (finem) (8,1–2, A). Philosophy concerns the visible or that which can be understood by the use of reason (intelligere sua ratione), while theology concerns the invisible or that which has to be believed above all reason (credibile supra omnem rationem) (7,28, A;33–36, C). According to Luther, the very point of the disputation is that God is not subject to reason and syllogisms (subiectus rationi et syllogismorum), but to the word of God and faith (8,4–5, A). Therefore faith is not restricted or subject to the rules or words of philosophy (regulis seu verbis philosophiæ adstricta aut subiecta), but is free with respect to it (7,36–37, C).

Theories of Consequences

In the following pages my purpose is to scrutinize »sophistical arguments» (argumentum sophisticum) (11,1, A) that are criticized by Luther, and to shed light on the conceptual presuppositions of his remarks. On the one hand, I will especially pay attention to what kind of philosophical tools Luther criticizes, and on the other hand, what kind of tools, if any, he himself applies in his criticism.[10]

---

[9] Luther's view is different here e.g. from that of Anselm of Canterbury who in his ontological argument connects the meanings of 'cogitare' and 'intelligere' so that to think something is to understand it. See *Kirjavainen,* 1983, 100. From Anselms's point of view one could not say that a person can think of a thing which is beyond his understanding. By »thinking» Luther seems to mean something approaching the idea that a person can by means of his reason operate any terms quite well, even though he actually does not understand them.

[10] Bengt Hägglund states that Luther's negative views on some questions under

The first argument deals with the question whether one can say in philosophy that from God's infinite power (infinita potentia) it follows that God became man. There are some differences between three *Handschriften* of the disputation. In text A the argument is in the form of the following hypothetical syllogism:

> Si philosophia tribuit Deo infinitam potentiam, videmur ei etiam tribuere hoc, quod verbum posset fieri caro.
>
> Sed philosophia tribuit Deo summam potentiam. Ergo tribuit etiam ei, quod verbum caro factum est. (8,10—12)

The argument is an inference of a form *modus ponens:* If p, then q. But p, therefore q. In text B the conclusion is drawn from one premiss only. *Philosophia tribuit Deo infinitam potentiam. Ergo tribuit etiam ei potentiam incarnationis. Antecendens probo ex definitione: Deus est mens aeterna infinita.* (8,24—26). On the other hand in text C there seems to be some kind of confusion between its premisses and the conclusion.

> Quicunque admittit Deo infinitam potentiam, ille etiam videtur tribuere verbo humanitatem.
>
> Sed philosophia admittit.
>
> Ergo omnes philosophi tribuunt Deo infinitam potentiam, ut Plato credit, Deum esse conditorem mundi. In hoc Aristotele maior. Concedunt Deo gubernanti infinitam potentiam, id est, mundum infinitum. (8,29—33)

In this case the conclusion is certainly not *ergo omnes philosophi tribuunt Deo potentiam infinitam,* which is included in the first premiss. Luther's response presupposes, however, that this argument also has the form *modus ponens.* In other words, whoever concedes to God infinite power, attributes humanity to the Word.

---

consideration in the disputation, for instance such as on the question of the possibility of the supernatural logic of faith, would rest on »purely theological grounds». *Hägglund,* 1955, 46. This is only partly true. Luther has undoubtedly important theological reasons for his position. But it does not mean that he would not also have some patterns of thinking or conceptual premises which direct his theological and philosophical standpoints. This fact especially concerns his notion of 'reason' (ratio). It is tempting to be contented with what Luther says about reason. However, it is more important to see what he himself understands by ratio. For example, *Lohse,* 1958, examines extensively and profoundly Luther's remarks about reason, its use in theology and its relation to religious belief (fides). Thus, »Luther's conception of reason» is to be understood as everything which Luther *says* about reason, and not what kind of conception of reason Luther's *own argumentation* actually presupposes.

The first argument argues against the second thesis, according to which it would be simply impossible and absurd (simpliciter impossibile et absurdum) in philosophy that the Word was made flesh. On the contrary, in theology the proposition »the Word was made flesh» is true. Luther answer to this argument is a twofold one. First, he wants to state that philosophers like Plato and Aristotle do not attribute to God infinite power (8,13–15, A;14,15–21, A). This counter-argument based on the history of philosophy (whether true or not, it is not of interest to us here) is not essential for Luther's point of view. What is essential, is that according to philosophy one cannot say that God is creator and created, or God is man, although one could say in philosophy God is *potentia infinita* (8,17–9,1, A).

By the expression *secundum philosophiam non potest dici* Luther clearly means that one cannot deduce from the philosophical concept of 'God' the incarnation. Such a deduction would be contradictory, not in fact to theology, but in the first place to philosophy itself, because in philosophy it is contradictory to say that God is both infinite and finite. If philosophy attributes humanity to God, it attributes something which it does not comprehend (14,31–35, C).

God is infinite, and therefore in philosophy one can by no means (nullo modo) concede that God can become man. Although one can (also in philosophy) think and say that God is omnipotent, nevertheless one cannot understand and establish that God was made man, because in that case the infinite would be contained in the finite. Therefore Luther says: »Nego consequentiam.» (9,1–4, A;19–21, B).

The second thesis and the responses given to its counter-arguments offer an example in which the statement *idem non est verum in theologia et philosophia* means the case that some proposition is true in theology, but impossible and absurd in philosophy. The proposition »God became man» is senseless in philosophy, because it cannot be understood. Therefore it cannot be said in philosophy. Quite a different case is offered by Luther's examples of syllogisms which are »good» (bonus) in philosophy, but false (falsus) in theology. Syllogisms of this kind are:

> Pater in divinis generat
> Pater est essentia divina
> Ergo essentia divina generat. (T16)

Omnis essentia divina est pater
Filius est essentia divina
Ergo filius est pater. (T18)

Quidquid factum est caro, factum est creatura
Filius Dei est factus caro
Ergo filius Dei est factus creatura. (T22)

Omnis caro est creatura
Verbum est caro
Ergo verbum est creatura. (T24)

Omnis caro est creatura
Verbum non est creatura
Ergo verbum non est caro. (T25)

Luther says about these kinds of syllogisms that there is *forma optima, sed nihil ad materiam* (T26). These syllogisms are true and good from a formal point of view (i.e. in philosophy or logic), but from the material point of view (i.e. in theology) false. Luther wants to make a definite distinction between the form and the matter of the syllogism. This can be seen very clearly from his response to the argument of Polonus (Hans Polner?). According to Polonus, the matter is that thing with which the form or syllogism deals (materia est illa res, de qua tractat forma seu syllogismus). If the error is in the matter, not in the form, it has to be either in the minor or major premiss. But this is not the case in the theses proposed by Luther. Therefore the error is not in the matter (9,32–36, C). On the contrary, in theses 17 and 19 both premisses are true (verae), but the conclusion is nevertheless false. So, from what is true follows what is false (ex vero sequitur falsum) and truth does not agree with truth (verum vero non consonat) which is *contra philosophiam.*

According to Luther, however, a syllogism in order to be a syllogism, does not imply that there could be no fault in its matter. It is the form of the syllogism which consists of the major premiss, the minor premiss and the conclusion. The matter is not yet included in these terms (materia non in hos terminos concluditur) (10,16–18, C). Luther obviously seems to think that the validity of a syllogism does not depend on its matter, but on its form. A syllogism is valid or »good» if it has a correct form, a major and minor premiss (i.e. three terms) and a conclusion.

Luther's remarks on the goodness of the syllogistic form can be cleared up by means of a discussion about the consequences (consequentiae) in medieval logic. In this discussion the term 'good' (bonus) had the explicit technical meaning indicating the validity of an inference. The notion of 'consequentia' included, however, seen from the logical point of view, inferential relationships of different kinds. First of all, it covered what in modern logic is meant by implication or a conditional proposition of the form 'if p, then q' (in which 'p' is the antecedent and 'q' the consequent). Secondly, it also included the case in which two propositions are related to each other in such a way that the former cannot be true without the latter being true as well (i.e. entailment or strict implication). The third use of the notion of consequence was connected with an argument, or an inference of the form 'p; therefore q', when the conclusion is drawn from the premiss (or premisses).[11]

The very fact that the notion of consequence covered all three of these relationships between propositions led to certain difficulties. One problem was, whether one should say that the consequence is true or false or valid or invalid.[12] This ambiguity followed from the fact that the consequence was thought of on the one hand as the proposition which is true, and on the other hand as the valid argument. The validity of consequence was usually indicated by such expressions as »valet consequentia» and »consequentia bona est». However, very often term 'bona' was used alternatively with the term 'vera'.[13]

This inconsistency between the uses of the terms 'good' and 'true'

---

[11] *Boh,* 1982, 300. The first treatises with the title »de consequentiis» were apparently composed around 1300. For instance, *Walter Burley*'s early De consequentiis (before 1302) is a loose list of rules rather than a systematic theory about the subject whereas two versions of his later treatise De puritate artis logicae (c. 1320 and 1330) are more systematic attempts. *Jean Buridan*'s Tractatus de consequentiis (after 1355) already presents a highly systematic exposition of the whole doctrine. The origins of the theory of consequences is a disputable question. The tradition of Topics has been presented by some scholars (Boehner, Moody) as one important source. Another possible origin arises from the discussion of the hypothetical syllogisms. *Green-Pedersen,* 1984, 265—266. Green-Pedersen himself stresses the latter origin, especially *Boethius'* De hypotheticis syllogismis, *Green-Pedersen,* 272. See also *Stump,* 1982, 273—299.

[12] *Boh,* 1982, 301.

[13] *Kneale & Kneale,* 1966, 277. Only much later was it made completely clear that a consequence is not a proposition, but a sequence of propositions the purpose of which is to be an instance of a rule justifying that sequence. For example, John of St. Thomas (1589—1644) explicitly states that consequences are not propositions, and consequently they are assessed not as true or false but as valid or invalid. *Ashworth,* 1974, 120.

can also clearly be seen in Luther's approach to his subject matter. The disputation starts from the issue whether the same is true in theology and in philosophy, a position which Luther wishes to deny. The meaning which he gives to the expression »idem est (non est) verum in theologia et philosophia», is not in the first place, whether the truth (veritas) is the same or whether the same proposition is true in both of them. On the contrary, Luther's very emphasis is in the question, whether the same *consequence* is true in theology and in philosophy. He may represent the nominalistic notion of truth, according to which 'true' is predicated of propositions, not of things. But Luther's most important point cannot be exhausted only by referring to the difference between the Aristotelian-Thomistic or metaphysical notion of truth and the nominalistic or propositional notion of truth, because all his examples of propositions which are true in philosophy but false in theology, are in fact conclusions of syllogistic arguments.[14]

In theories of consequence the question about the validity of an argument, and the truth of a conditional corresponding to it, were very closely related to each other. The conditional was regularly understood as the strict implication or as the necessary connection between the antecedent and the consequent. For instance, *Petrus Hispanus* defines the true conditional necessary and the false conditional impossible in his Summule Logicales as follows: *veritatem conditionalis exigitur quod antecedens non possit esse verum sine consequenti, ut 'si homo est, animal est'. Unde omni conditionalis vera est necessaria, et omnis conditionalis falsa est impossibilis.*[15] The interpretation of the conditional as a necessary relationship between the antecedent and the consequent implies that

---

[14] Hägglund may be right when stressing that Luther's conception of truth is by nature a nominalistic one. Truth is a property of a proposition, not of »being» (ens et verum convertuntur). However, in his disputation Luther is examining the whole question from the viewpoint of the logical consequence. Therefore, a mere reference to the propositional conception of truth by Nominalists does not yet shed light on Luther's line of thought. Cf. *Hägglund,* 1955, 90—96. On the scholastic theories of truth, see *Boehner,* 1958, 174—200. Luther apparently knew of the theory of consequences through his teacher in logic, *Jodocus Trutvetter* from Eisenach (Isennacensis) (Breviarium dialecticum, Erphord 1500, Summule totius logicae, Erphord 1501). Trutvetter was familiar with the logical works of Ockham, Buridan, Marsilius of Inghen and Albert of Saxony. See *Asworth,* 1974, X. On Trutwetter's logic in this respect, see *Kleineidam,* 1969, 149—151. See also footnote 18.

[15] *Petrus Hispanus,* 1972, I, 9,15—18.

every time when there is a true conditional of the form 'if p, then q' there is also a valid argument of the form 'p; therefore q' corresponding to it. This is not the case if the conditional is taken as a so called material (or truth functional) implication.[16]

One important distinction made in theories of consequence is that between a *formal* and a *material* consequence. For instance according to *Pseudo-Scotus,* the former holds for all terms by virtue of the similar order and form of the terms (quae tenet in omnibus terminis stante consimili dispositione et forma terminorum). The form of the consequence consists of categorematic terms (i.e. predicate and subject terms), syncategorematic terms (indicating e.g. conjunction, disjunction, universality or particularity), copula (either indicative 'de inesse' or modal 'de modo') and the premisses (affirmative or negative).[17]

On the other hand, the material consequence does not hold by virtue of its form, but because of the meaning of the terms included in it. Any material consequence can be reduced to a formal consequence by taking into consideration the unexpressed additional premiss. If this additional premiss indicates that there is a necessary connection between the antecedent and the consequent, the consequence in question is *consequentia materialis vera (bona) simpliciter.* If this additional premiss is by nature contingent, the consequence in question is *consequentia vera (bona) ut nunc.* For example, the material consequence *Homo currit, ergo animal currit* is true and good *simpliciter,* because it can be reduced to the formal consequence by means of the additional premiss *Omnis homo est animal* which displays the necessary relationship between the terms 'homo' and 'animal'. On the contrary, the consequence *Sortes currit, ergo albus currit* is true and good *ut nunc,* because the additional premiss *Sortes est albus* is contingent, not necessary.[18]

---

[16] *Boh,* 1982, 302.

[17] *Kneale & Kneale,* 1966, 278—279. *(Pseudo-Scotus,* Quaestiones super libros Priorum.).

[18] *Kneale & Kneale,* 1966, 288. See also *Green-Pedersen,* 1984, 266—267, 290—291. There were various definitions about formal and material consequence. Two definitions of quite a different kind prevailed. According to one the consequent is included or understood in the antecedent. On the other hand, the material consequence is defined as that in which this inclusion does not occur. This definition was shared by many 14th century logicians in England (e.g. Robert Fland, Richard Lavenham, Ralph Strode). But on the continent a new kind of definition was given. According to this, the formal consequence is valid by virtue of its form irrespective

William Ockham in the third part of his Summa Logicae also makes the same kind of distinction in the form *consequentia simplex* and *consequentia ut nunc.*[19] The consequence is simplex when the antecedent can never be (pro nullo tempore) true without the consequent being true as well. But it is ut nunc when the antecedent is sometimes (pro aliquo tempore) true without the consequent being true. Ockham makes a further distinction between a consequence which holds *per medium extrinsecum,* and a consequence which holds *per medium intrinsecum.* The latter holds by means of a proposition which has been formed from the same terms expressed in the consequence in question. For example, the consequence *Sortes non currit, igitur homo non currit* only holds because the proposition *Sortes est homo,* formed of the same terms, is true. Without this proposition being true, the consequence in question would not be valid (non valeret).

On the contrary, the consequence *per medium extrinsecum* holds, not by virtue of the terms, but by virtue of some general rule (per aliquam regulam generalem), like the consequence *Tantum homo est asinus, igitur omnis asinus est homo.* In other words, it is valid by virtue of some logical rule, which in this example permits the syncategorematic terms 'tantum' and 'omnis' to change and to move from the exclusive proposition to the universal one (Ad exclusiva ad universalem de terminis transpositis est bona consequentia).[20]

By means of this distinction Ockham defines the difference between the formal and material consequence. The formal consequence holds either mediately or immediately per medium extrinsecum, depending on the form of the propositions alone. By the »form» Ockham means along with other scholastics (there is no difference between realists and

---

of the signification of its terms, i.e. *in omni materia.* Any consequence regardless of which terms occur in it, is valid if it has the correct form (i.e. for purely syntactic reasons). The material consequence is valid only in a certain matter or is valid because of the signification of the terms occurring in it (i.e. for semantic reasons). For instance, Jean Buridan, Marsilius of Inghen, the Pseudo-Scotus and Albert of Saxone are representatives of this conception. *Green-Pedersen,* 1984, 287—288. Luther apparently knew of this latter definition through Trutwetter. See footnote 14 above.

[19] *Boehner,* 1958, 334.

[20] *Boehner,* 1958, 334—338. The consequence which holds *per medium intrinsecum* is by nature so called *enthymema* or an imperfect syllogism because one premiss is lacking in it. If this lacking premiss is inserted a perfect syllogism is produced. *Ibid.,* 338—339. See also *Stump,* 1982, 282—283.

nominalists on this point) the structure of the propositions, which is determined by the positions of the categorematic and syncategorematic terms. The cyncategorematic terms as logical terms belong to the form, and the categorematic terms to the matter (materia). By the material consequence Ockham means a consequence which holds by reason of the terms (ratione terminorum) included in it, not by virtue of the logical form. Ockham takes as his examples the consequences *Si homo est, Deus est* and *Homo est asinus, igitur Deus non est.* The former is always true, because the consequent is always true. The latter is also true, because the antecedent is always false.[21]

Ratio and Syllogistic Form

Luther's conception seems clearly to imply that the Trinitarian and Christological syllogisms in question are »good», and in this sense also true in philosophy, when they are taken as formal syllogisms. They hold »by virtue of the order and form of the terms» (Pseudo-Scotus) and by virtue of logical rules concerning the structure of the syllogism or »per medium extrinsecum» (Ockham). In this case, however, the meaning of the categorematic terms of these syllogisms i.e. their *materia* has been overlooked. They have been taken in a way as mere term variables. Luther rejects the claim that the syllogistic form, although being in itself good and without defect, should actually hold *in omnibus terminis,* when the meaning or *materia* of terms has been taken into consideration. As soon as the meaning of the terms are considered, for example the term 'homo', the syllogisms in question become »sophistical arguments» (11,1, A).

Therefore Luther can consistently say: *Est bona forma, sed conclusio falsa.* (20,12, A). He does not reject these formulations as such or he does not question the validity of the syllogistic form in general, because it is not a fault of the syllogistic form but of the virtue and majesty of the matter of the terms included in them (T20; 18,11—12, A). For the same reason we can say that Luther is not representing a double truth theory, because when arguing that *idem non est verum in theologia et philosophia* he only states that a syllogism in philosophy can be formal-

---

[21] *Boehner,* 1958, 339—343. Appealing to these examples Boehner has tried to show that Ockham in fact knew of the idea of the material implication. *Boehner,* 1958, 342—351. See also *Adams,* 1972.

ly good and true, and notwithstanding this can at the same time in theology be »materially» false. This can be seen quite clearly from the following response in which Luther's ambigious use of 'true' is obvious. *Nos negamus, principia dialectica esse vera in hac materia, et dicimus, quod non idem verum sit in theologia et philosophia* (12,17—18, A).[22]

In the logic of the 13th and 14th century, particularly in the commentaries on Aristotle's De Sophisticis Elenchis it was disputed whether a syllogism with faulty matter or false premisses is actually a syllogism at all. For instance, *Simon of Faversham* (Simon Anglicus c. 1260—1306/7) in his treatise Quaestiones super libro elenchorum in question 7 asks *Utrum syllogismus peccans in materia vel syllogismus ex falsis sit syllogismus.* Simon finds that there are different opinions among »the ancients» and »the moderns» (apud antiquos et apud modernos) about this issue. Simon himself, however, states that *syllogismus peccans in materia* is a syllogism.[23] On the other hand, *syllogismus peccans in forma* is not a syllogism, because it violates the general conditions of a syllogism. Just as something cannot be a man without the form of man, so something cannot be a syllogism without the form of a syllogism. The expression *syllogismus peccans in forma* does not imply that there is such a syllogism, but instead it implies *oppositum in adiecto.*[24]

According to Luther the Christological syllogism *Omnis homo est creatura. Christus est homo. Ergo Christus est creatura* is by nature

---

[22] Hägglund also says that Luther does not represent the »double truth theory,» but he fails to see the most central reason for this. Cf. *Hägglund,* 1955, 93—94.

[23] *Simon of Faversham,* 1984, 48,33. Quaestiones veteres, q.7. »Item hoc dicit (Aristoteles) hic in illo capitulo 'Quoniam autem habemus' (Analytica Posteriora) quod syllogismus falsus est dupliciter, vel qui falso syllogizat, vel quia falsum syllogizat. Ille autem qui falsum syllogizat est peccans in materia. Cum enim peccans in materia est syllogismus. Manifestum est ergo quod peccans in materia est syllogismus.» 48,105—109.

[24] »Nunc autem omnis syllogismus peccans in forma peccat contra condiciones generales syllogismi.». . . »Ideo syllogismus peccans in forma non est syllogismus.» *Simon of Faversham,* 1984, 112,31—33, 38—39. Quaestiones novae, q.5. »Non enim dicitur aliquis esse homo, nisi habeat formam hominis. Ideo sic debet esse in syllogismo quod nihil debet dici syllogismus nisi illud quod habet formam syllogismi.» 112,44—46. »Et ideo sicut non sequitur 'homo mortuus; ergo homo' sic nec sequitur 'syllogismus peccans in forma; ergo syllogismus' sed dicendo 'syllogismus peccans in forma' est oppositum in adiecto.» 112,51—53.

argumentum sophisticum (10,4–5, A; 11,1, A). Also Luther's answer to the question: »Whether *syllogismus peccans in materia* is a syllogism?» is affirmative. But a syllogism which violates the conditions of the syllogistic form of minor and major premiss and conclusion (forma autem est maior, minor et conclusio) (10,16–17, C) is not a syllogism, because »where is neither major nor minor premiss, there is no syllogism» (11,2–3, A). So, on this point his view seems to be parallel with Simon of Faversham.

As we found at the beginning of this paper Luther regards as the main point of his disputation the fact that God is not subject to reason and syllogisms (8,5, A). The difference between philosophy and theology lies in the fact that the former concerns that which one can understand by reason (intelligere sua ratione), while the latter concerns that which one can only believe above all reason (supra omnem rationem). Faith is not confined and subject to the rules and words of philosophy, it is free from them (7,34–37, C). Luther seems to identify reason (ratio) with the syllogistic form. In thesis 20 he says *expressis verbis* that the matter in Trinitarian and Christological syllogisms is by nature such that »one cannot include it within the narrow limits of reason or syllogisms» (rationis seu syllogismorum).

On this point Luther is representing the common medieval conception according to which the rules of logic are rules which reason itself has abstracted from its own action. They are rules which reason follows with natural necessity. For instance, Thomas Aquinas says in his commentary on Aristotle's Analytica Posteriora, that »as the intellect understands itself, so the reason can ratiocinate from its own action (ratio de suo actu ratiocinari potest)». Therefore a particular science (ars) is needed, which concerns the acts of reason. This science is logic or *rationalis scientia*.[25] In Aristotelian metaphysics and in the theory of science built on it, the formal structures of reason and reality are uniform, for the acts of reason are similar to the acts of nature (actus rationis similes sunt actibus naturae).[26]

---

[25] *Opera omnia* 4, 273,n.1—n.2.

[26] *Opera omnia* 4, 273,n.5. It was a common view since the beginning of the 11th century, often accepted without discussion, that language, thought and reality have the same logical structure and coherence. For instance, language was taken to be not only an instrument of thought, expression and communication but an important

Syllogismus demonstrativus which affects scientific knowledge (syllogismus faciens scire), can do it only because reason and reality have the same syllogistic structure. Therefore it was customary to presume that the whole of intelligible thinking gains its virtual power in syllogism and from syllogism, and can finally be reduced to a syllogism. This concerns both demonstrative and dialectical syllogisms. They do not differ from each other in the form, but in the matter. In demonstrative syllogisms the relationships between terms are necessary, while in dialectical syllogisms they are only probable.[27]

Luther does not seem to question this common view in any substantial way, although he wants to limit the scope of reason to the visible world only. Everything which is visible and an object of philosophy can be understood *sua ratione,* can also be expressed by means of material and formal syllogistic inference and argument. On the other hand, that which is invisible and has to be believed as an object of theology *supra omnem rationem,* cannot be expressed by means of formal and material syllogisms. In the syllogisms in question the propositions occurring as premisses are true, but one cannot form syllogisms by means of them. According to Luther, they can be tested only by the word of God *sine syllogismo,* without philosophy or logic. Philosophy has nothing to do with the grammar of the word of God. *Philosophia nihil in grammatica nostra* (12,5–8, A).

The principles of logic are not valid or »true» in theological matter (12,17, A). There is no major or minor premiss in the matter of theological propositions (in materia non est neque maior neque minor). But where one cannot find a major or a minor premiss, there is no syllogism (ubi non est maior nec minor, ibi non est syllogismus). Therefore according to Luther, »the form without matter can be rejected» (potest reiici forma sine materia) (11,1–4, A). In general, a syllogism is a syllogism without matter, when it has *bona forma,* but without matter there is no formal syllogistic argument or consequence. From the material or theological point of view syllogistic arguments consisting of Christological and Trinitarian terms turn out to be fallacies. *Sunt syllogismi boni i dialectica, in theologia non.* (23,1, A).

---

source of information concerning reality. Hence, logico-semantic and metaphysical viewpoints were completely interwoven. *L.M. De Rijk,* 1982, 161.

[27] *Stump,* 1982, 284.

The formally good syllogism *Omnis homo est creatura. Christus est homo. Ergo Christus est creatura* proves from the material point of view to be a fallacy, because the middle term 'homo' is equivocal in the minor premiss (Christus est homo).[28] Consequently, there are actually four terms in this syllogism, not three. Therefore the syllogism in question is no longer formally good or it is not a syllogism at all. In the major premiss (omnis homo est creatura) the term 'homo' signifies the physical man (hominem physicum), while in the minor premiss divine and incarnate God (divinum et incarnatum Deum) (10,34–11,27–29, C; 11,8–10, A). In this case 'homo' does not signify in the same manner as in the tree of Porphyrius. It signifies something greater and higher *extra arborem Porphyriam* (12,4–10, A). Because Luther actually seems to identify reason with the syllogistic form, it follows that theological propositions, when they depart from the syllogistic form, also depart from reason.

Philosophy and theology are not, however, contrary to each other. The matter of theological propositions is not *contra veritatem dialecticam,* but above and outside it (supra, extra) (T21). In order that a contrariety (contrarietas) and a contradiction (contradictoria) could be considered, terms and propositions have to belong to the same genus. It is not so, however, in this case. According to Luther, it is quite clear that »God» and »man» do not mean the same for pagan philosophers as for theology. In philosophy the proposition »Deus est homo» is another (alia) proposition than in theology. In the former it is false, while in the latter true. Therefore it is necessary to separate these spheres from each other (16,8–13, A). One cannot build the syllogistic argument upon these propositions, because *nihil valet argumentatio, quia ambiqua non debent poni in syllogismo* (11,15–16, A).

This casts more light on Luther's distinction between »believing», »understanding» and »thinking». To understand something means to Luther that the thing in question can be put into the form of the syllogistic reasoning and argument. However, one cannot understand theological

---

[28] Referring to Pierre d'Ailly Luther says as early as in his Christmas Sermon (1515): »...omnis syllogismus ex terminis divinis, qui infert conclusionem falsam, certissime peccat secundum Fallaciam aequivocationis vel Figurae dictionis. Et hinc fit, ut non omnes propositiones divinae possint intrare formam Syllogisticam, et si intrant, faciunt hanc Fallaciam,...». WA 1, 22,9—13.

propositions in this sense of »understanding», because to understand is to infer a proposition (as a conclusion) from other propositions (as premisses) within the syllogistic form. Therefore one cannot conclude from theological propositions that they are true (concludere, quod vera sint, ex sese non potest) (15,6, A). One can »think» them in the sense that one can build upon them formally good syllogisms, but materially or theologically they are empty, or *nihil ad materiam* (T26).

Supernatural Logica Fidei

One possible way to solve this dilemma, a way which is however refused by Luther, would be to question the universal validity of the syllogistic form and to develop some kind of supernatural logic. In fact, one can see in the 14th century logic a particular crisis which concerned precisely this question about the universal validity of the syllogistic formality.[29] The scholastic conception of logic was essentially formal. The syllogistic rules were tought to guarantee that the syllogistic form necessarily gives a true conclusion whenever the variables have been replaced by suitable categorematic terms, notwithstanding the matter of terms and propositions. For instance, the unknown author of the *Centiloquium,* referring to this principle of Aristotle says that no discourse is formal if the terms can be invented by which the premisses of the syllogism are true but its conclusion false. This doctrine was commonly accepted by the Scholastics.[30]

This kind of problematic situation, however, is brought forth when Trinitarian (and Christological) terms are introduced into the discourse. In the syllogisms compiled by them the premisses are true, but the conclusions false. As regards the universal validity of the syllogistic form, the author of the Centiloquium is a representative of logical skepticism. According to him, the syllogisms compiled by Trinitarian terms offer a representative counter-example to show that the syllogistic formality is not universally valid. Such a case is, for example, the *syllogismus expositorius* as follows.

> Haec essentia est Pater
> Haec essentia est Filius
> Ergo Filius est Pater

---

[29] Boehner, 1958, 351.
[30] *Boehner,* 1958, 353—355. The *Centiloquium,* Concl. 56a, 272.

Both premisses of this syllogism are true, though the conclusion is still false. The syllogisms of the first figure are not universally valid either, as the syllogisms *de omni* and *de nullo* of the following kind display.

Omnis essentia divina est Pater
Omnis Filius in divinis est essentia divina
Ergo omnis Filius in divinis est Pater

Nullus Filius in divinis est Pater in divinis
Haec essentia est Filius in divinis
Ergo haec essentia non est Pater in divinis

Again in both syllogisms the premisses are true but the conclusion is nevertheless false. Therefore neither of these formal consequences is valid because they violate the rule: *Ab inferiori ad superius affirmativae sine distributione, consequentia valet.*[31] The author of the Centiloquium is not only content with disputing the formality of syllogistic logic and its universal validity, but he wants to replace it with supernatural logic. Logic can still be formal and universally valid by formulating an additional rule based on a supernaturally invented discourse (discursus supernaturaliter inventus) or on revelation. Thus, for example, the true premisses *Iste Pater in divinis generat* and *Iste Pater in divinis est essentia divina* do not lead to the conclusion *Essentia divina generat*. The correct conclusion is *Aliqua persona, quae est essentia divina, generat* or *Aliquis, qui est essentia divina, generat.* This is possible by taking into considera-

---

[31] *Boehner,* 1958, 355—356. Boehner's main argument against Ockham being the author of the Centiloquium (as Erwin Iserloh has stated), is founded on the fact that Ockham does not question the formality and validity of syllogistic logic. On the contrary, he with other Scholastics vindicates the formal nature of logic. The *syllogismus expositorius* (or the syllogism which has two singular premisses arranged according to the third figure and in which the conclusion is either singular or particular or indefinite, but never universal) is valid irrespective of the matter. According to Ockham, however, the Trinitarian syllogismus expositorius (Haec essentia est Pater, etc.) does not satisfy these conditions for the premisses. A subject term of the singular premiss is to supposit only for one thing, not several things. Therefore the syllogismus expositorius is not valid for the Trinitarian terms. The same concerns also the syllogisms de omni and de nullo. 'Omnis essentia divina est Pater' does not actually allow that everything which can be predicated of divine essence could be predicated of 'Father'. Consequently it is not in fact syllogismus de omni. *Boehner,* 1958, 359—362. See *Ockham,* 1954, IaIIIae, c.16,1—6; 9—38; c.4,150—177. Boehner thinks that the Centiloquium has been brought forth not in the neighborhood of Ockham, but rather in the neighborhood of Robert Holkot. *Ibid.,* 370—372.

tion the additional rule concerning Trinity and which says that *Pater est alius a Filio et Filius est alius a Patre, non tamen aliud.* This makes a distinction between the masculine gender 'alius' and the neuter gender 'aliud'. Father is *aliud suppositum a Filio,* it is not *aliud a Filio,* but it is *alius a Filio.* Only the masculine or feminine gender can be used with the personal subject, a neuter cannot be used.[32]

It is interesting to see that in the 29th argument of the disputation Luther appeals to the same distinction when saying *Pater est alius, non aliud, sic filius est alius, non aliud.* According to Luther, in theology one has to speak in *genere masculino,* not in *genere neutro* (28,11–17, A).[33] Holy Trinity is *tres disctinctae personae,* but still *una essentia.* However, Luther takes another stand as the author of the Centiloquium, because this can never be understood by human reason (intelligi a ratione humana); but it has to be believed (24,11–12, A).[34]

As we have already shown, Luther does not question the formality and validity of syllogistic logic, as the author of the Centiloquium does. The syllogismus expositorius, *Pater in divinis generat. Pater est essentia divina. Ergo essentia divina generat* is »good» (bonus) or formally valid.

---

[32] *Boehner,* 1958, 357; See the *Centiloquium,* Concl. 59a,273—274, 57a,271.

[33] Luther's remark is not connected with the Centiloquium. He refers to the first book of the Sentences of Petrus Lombardus, in which Petrus says: »Dicit tamen Augustinus in epistola *Ad Maximum* quod Pater se alterum genuit, his verbis: 'Pater, ut haberet Filium de se ipso, non minuit se ipsum, sed ita genuit de se alterum se, ut totus maneret in se et esset in Filio tantus, quantus et solus'. Quod ita intelligi potest: id est de se alterum genuit, non utique alterum Deum, sed alteram personam; vel genuit se alterum, id est genuit alterum qui est hoc quod ipse; nam etsi alius sit Pater quam Filius, non est tamen aliud, sed unum.» *Petrus Lombardus,* 1981, 1b I, dist.IV, c2(14), 80,15—22. See also Luther's Christmas Sermon (1515), WA 1, 21,35—22,6.

[34] Luther takes mathematics to be the worst enemy of theology. No other area of philosophy contends with theology as much as mathematics when it argues that one cannot be two, and three cannot be one, as in the article of the Trinity. The same concerns the Sacrament of the Altar. The mathematician does not believe that the bread and the wine is the body and the blood of Christ. According to Luther, mathematics ought to remain in its own sphere and place (debet manere in sua sphaera et loco). »Three cannot be one» is the firmest demonstration (certissima demonstratio), but it is so only *extra theologiam.* Therefore, mathematics ought to keep within in its own sphere and to dispute the unity and the trinity in its own way (suo modo). 22,29—32; 23,20—21,C.

On the other hand, although in the thesis 27 he says that »in articles of faith one must have recourse to another logic and philosophy (ad aliam dialecticam et philosophiam),» he unambigiously refuses the very idea of the particular logic of faith. Luther's attitude does not deviate here from what he had already said in his early disputation *Contra scholasticam theologiam* (1517).[35] In this disputation Luther objects to »modern logicians» because they vainly fabricate a »logic of faith», *logica fidei, Suppositio mediata extra terminum et numerum* (T46). In the next thesis he argues against Pierre d'Ailly (Cardinalis Cameracensis) that »no syllogistic form holds in the divine terms» (T47). Hence, it does not follow that the article of Trinity would contradict (repugnere) the syllogistic form (T48). But, if the syllogistic form (forma syllogistica) would hold for the divine terms, then the article of Trinity would not be believed, but it would be known (T49).[36]

Luther and the Logic of Terms

In the disputation under consideration Luther also refuses Pierre d'Ailly's effort to restore Trinitarian propositions to the sphere of rational discourse by means of the terminist logic. According to Luther, in matters

[35] WA 1, 224—228.

[36] Hägglund argues that Luther just by his critical attitude to supernatural logic takes a stand against the Nominalists and severs his connections with the Occamistic tradition. *Hägglund,* 1955, 53—54. He seems to suppose that the very idea of supernatural logic is expressly peculiar to Nominalism and Occamism. This not the case, as Boehner has shown regarding Ockham. See footnote 31 above. It is true, however, that *Biel* takes a positive attitude towards the Trinitarian logic of d'Ailly. Biel critizes Gregory of Rimini who does not present correctly Ockham's point of view. Sent.I, dist.5, qu.1, dub.3,F. See *Greg. Arim.* Sent.I, dist.5, qu.1, 53N. On Luther's criticism in the disputation Contra scholasticam theologiam, see *Maierù,* 1986. In this article Maierù deals with the question what Luther means when he criticizing logic of faith says: »suppositio mediata extra terminum et numerum.» Maierù suggests that Luther's thesis 46 is defective and that there should be »distributio extra terminum et numerum.» However, neither Biel nor d'Ailly use such a phrase. Biel, for example, uses the phrase »distributio completa/non completa.» On the contrary, Henricus Totting de Oyta and Petrus de Bruxellis use the phrase »distributio extra terminum et numerum.» However, Maierù does not refer to Trutvetter. In fact the phrase in question can be found in Trutvetter's Summule totius logicae, where he makes a distinction between »distributio in termino,» »distributio extra terminum,» and »distributio extra numerum.» Pars prima, cap. 3, de suppositione in genere.

of faith one must neither use nor utilize such subtle inventions of terminist logic as immediate and mediate supposition (suppositio immediata et mediata) (T12). Luther seems on the whole to take a negative attitude towards the discussion about the properties of terms (proprietates terminorum) and terminist logic. The extremely important notion of the logic of terms, i.e. *suppositio,* appears infrequently in his writings, and when it does, usually in bad light.[37]

The theory of properties of terms was purposed to display those possible roles a word can play, when it is used as a term in a proposition.[38] For instance, Petrus Hispanus defines supposition in his Summule Logicales as follows. *Suppositio est acceptio termini substantivi pro aliquo.* Supposition is not identical with signification. Signification is brought about *per impositionem vocis ad rem significandam,* while supposition is »acceptance of a term already significative of a thing for something.» Therefore signification is prior to supposition, for »significare» is a property of a word, while »supponere» is a property of a term which is composed of word and signification (compositi ex voce et significatione).[39]

The following scheme presents his division of supposition:[40]

SUPPOSITIO

1a) communis   b) discreta

2a) naturalis   b) accidentalis

3a) simplex   b) personalis

4a) determinata   b) confusa

5a) mobilis   b) immobilis

1a)   suppositio communis; e.g. the term 'homo'
b)   suppositio discreta; 'Sortes', 'iste homo'

---

[37] See for instance, WA 1, 21,38—22,5; 22,9—13. On other occurrences of the term 'supposition' by Luther, see WA 1, 77,21—26, WA 6, 510,25—30; 511,3—6; WA 9, 40,34—41,2; 58,30—33. According to De Rijk the origin of terminist logic can be found in theories of fallacies and the grammatical theories of the 12th century. See *De Rijk,* 1962, 1967, 1982.

[38] *Kneale & Kneale,* 1966, 247.

[39] *Petrus Hispanus,* 1972, VI,3; 80,8—16.

[40] *Petrus Hispanus,* 1972, VI,4—9; 80—83. On various divisions of supposition in different theories, see *Spade,* 1982, 188—196; *Enders,* 1975, 56—102.

2a) suppositio naturalis; 'homo' when it supposits for all men in the past, present and future
  b) suppositio accidentalis; 'homo erit,' 'homo est,' 'homo fuit,' when 'homo' supposits for men separately in the past, present or future
3a) suppositio simplex; 'homo est species,' 'animal est genus'
  b) suppositio personalis; 'homo currit'
4a) suppositio determinata; 'homo currit,' 'aliquis homo currit'
  b) suppositio confusa; 'omnis homo est animal'
5a) suppositio mobilis; 'omnis homo, ergo Sortes' or when it is possible to descend from universal to particular
  b) suppositio immobilis; 'omnis homo est animal,' from which it is not possible to descend to particular e.g. 'ergo omnis homo est hoc animal.'

William Ockham also says in his Summa Logicae that supposition is a property of a term (proprietas conveniens termino), and it has this property only in a proposition.[41] Supposition deals essentially with the truth of a proposition, and it is concerned with the following general principle: »Any term when it has signification never supposits in a proposition for something if this term cannot truly be predicated of it.»[42] First Ockham makes a difference between personal, simplex and material supposition. *Suppositio personalis* always occurs when »a term supposits for the thing it signifies, whether that thing be an entity outside the soul, a spoken word, an intention of the soul, a written word, or any other thing imaginable.» For example, *Omnis homo est animal, Omnis nomen vocale est pars orationis, Omnis species est universalis, Omnis intentio animae est in anima* are all personal suppositions, because the terms 'homo', 'nomen vocale', 'species' and 'intentio animae' in each proposition supposit for the thing they signify.[43]

---

[41] »Dicto de significationibus terminorum, restat dicere de suppositione, quae est proprietas conveniens termino, sed numquam nisi in propositione.» *Ockham,* 1951, Ia, c63,1—3.

[42] »Est igitur una regula generalis, quod numquam terminus in aliqua propositione, saltem quando significative accipitur, supponit pro aliquo, nisi de quo predicatur vere.» *Ockham,* 1951, Ia, c63,35—37.

[43] *Ockham,* 1951, Ia, c64,9—19. According to Ockham, »for the truth of a proposition is required that the subject term and the predicate term supposit for the same thing.» *Ockham,* 1951, IIa, c8,6—8. — Peter Geach has argued that this »two name theory» of Ockham together with his nominalism leads inevitably to an unorthodox Nestorianism in Christology, because two nature of Christ cannot be united in the way that Christ still could be one person or *suppositum. Geach,* 1972, 289—301. *Adams,* 1982, 62—75, has argued against Geach as has *Freddoso,* 1983, 293—330.

A term has *suppositio simplex* or *materialis* only when it is coupled in a proposition with another term or an extreme (comparatur alteri extremo), which refers to an intention of the soul, a spoken word or a written word. For instance, in the proposition *Homo currit* the term 'homo' cannot have simple or material supposition, because the term 'currit' does not refer to anything of this kind. On the contrary, in the proposition *Homo est species* the term 'homo' has suppositio simplex, because the term 'species' refers to the intention of the soul. The proposition *Sapientia est attributum Dei* is true, when it is seen as a simple supposition, but false if it is seen as a personal supposition. *Sortes est nomen, Homo est disyllaba* are examples of material supposition, because the terms in these propositions refer either to a spoken word or a written word.[44]

Thereafter Ockham makes further distinction within personal supposition as follows:[45]

SUPPOSITIO

personalis   simplex   materialis

discreta communis

determinata confusa

tantum distributiva

mobilis immobilis

Pierre d'Ailly's attempt to solve logical problems concerning Trinitarian paralogisms is based on a distinction within personal supposition.

On Ockhams's Christology, see also *Oberman,* 1963, 249—258. Ockham deals with this issue in his commentary on the Sentences in question 1, »Utrum solus Filius univit sibi naturam humanam in unitate suppositi«, and in question 10, »Utrum haec sit concedenda: Deus factus est homo«. *Ockham,* 1982, 3—42, 317—350. In question 10 he starts from the position that »ad veritatem propositionis affirmativae, quando uterque terminus ponitur in recto, requitur quod subiectum et predicatum supponat pro eodem.« *Ockham,* 1982, q.10, 317,7—9. On Luther's way of approaching problems concerning Christological formulas in the disputation under consideration and in the disputation *De divinitate et humanitate Christi,* 1540, (WA 39,II, 92—121), see for example *Mostert,* 1983, Band I, 350—359; *Schwarz,* 1966, 288—351; *Lienhard,* 1979, 244—264.

[44] *Ockham,* 1951, Ia, c65,6—13.
[45] *Ockham,* 1951, Ia, c69—c71.

According to d'Ailly, the terms *in divinis* have two kinds of supposition. The term 'Pater' supposits for Father mediately in divine essence (mediate pro patre in divinis), because it only covers to some extent the signification of the term 'essentia divina'. From this follows that not everything which is true of divine essence, is true of Father. For example, 'Son' can be predicated of divine essence, whereas 'Son' cannot be predicated of 'Father'. On the other hand, the term 'Pater' supposits immediately *pro patre in divinis* for that 'which produces, but is not produced' (pro re quae producit et non producitur) or its own signification. In this case 'Father' and 'which produces, but is not produced' are convertible with each other (qui convertitur conversione regulata per hoc signum omnis res quae est).[46]

The divine terms 'Pater,' 'Filius,' 'Spiritus Sanctus,' 'essentia divina' supposit immediately when they supposit for *omnis res quae est,* or when they cover completely that for which they personally supposit i.e. their signification; 'Pater' or 'which in divine essence produces, but is not produced,' 'Filius' or 'which in divine essence is produced, but does not produce' and 'Spiritus Sanctus' or 'which in divine essence does not produce and is not produced.' On the other hand, they supposit only mediately when they do not completely cover that for which they supposit, as the terms 'Pater', 'Filius' and 'Spiritus Sanctus' when they supposit for divine essence.[47]

Concluding Remarks

I have purported above to show some important conceptual and logical presuppositions in Luther's thinking to explain why he adopts particu-

---

[46] *Hägglund,* 1955, 45—46, footnote 55. See also *Maierù,* 1984.

[47] See *Hägglund,* 1955, 47—53. Also *Gabriel Biel* utilizes d'Ailly's distinction between the mediate and immediate supposition in question *Utrum Pater et Filius sunt unum principium spirans Spiritum Sanctum.* The term *principium* can be understood in twofold sense. When one says, like *Augustinus* in the *De Trinitate, Tres personae sunt unum principium creaturae,* the term *principium* supposits essentially (essentialiter), i.e. it supposits immediately for the divine essence. But in the proposition *Pater et Filius sunt unum principium Spiritus Sancti* the term *principium* does not suppose essentially because it is false to say *Pater et Filius sunt una essentia spirans.* On the contrary, it supposits immediately for the person. *Biel,* Sent. I, dist.12, qu1, art.3, dub.1,K. See also dub.4,N,0, where Biel quotes the relevant passage in d'Ailly's commentary on Sentences (Sent. I, qu5, art.2, not.3,M,N).

larly in the case of Trinitarian and Christological formulas a definite position towards the relationships between theology and philosophy. This position is founded on his view about the essential difference between theological and philosophical language. Luther seems to rest quite unambiguously on the scholastic standard conception of the formal validity of syllogistic logic. This explains why the form of Trinitarian and Christological syllogisms is said to be *bona,* although, seen from the theological or material point of view, contrary to the rules of logic the false conclusion would follow from the true premises. When these syllogisms are said to be good in philosophy and in this unqualified sense are also said to be true, it is possible for Luther to claim that what is true in philosophy does not need to be true in theology.

However, when these syllogisms are said to be good and true in philosophy, the meaning or the matter of their terms have actually been ignored. Because the valid formal consequence understood as the valid syllogistic argument presupposes both the form and the matter, and because those divine terms have the correct matter only in theology, Trinitarian and Christological propositions fall in the end outside of formal discourse. When Luther furthermore presupposes that human reason (ratio humana) and its acts essentially have the syllogistic structure and form, it follows that theological propositions also fall outside of human reason. Consequently, logic or philosophy is no use to theology or as Luther says: *Syllogismus non admittitur in mysteriis fidei et theologiae. Philosophia est error in theologia* (12,29–30, C).[48]

This conceptual background explains why Luther comes to the idea that *vox philosophica* like 'homo' is actually »a new word» (novum vocabulum) in theology. It does not signify and does not supposit for »fictious philosophical person», but *personam divinam sustentantem nostram humanam* (10,26–31, C). Thus, the word of God has its own *proprietas verbi* (19,9, A), which cannot rationally be based on or

---

[48] Already in his letter to Spalatine (1518) Luther (referring to his letter to Trutvetter which unfortunately has disappeared afterwards) says: »Scripsi denique ad d. Isennacensem, nostra etate (ut videtur) principem dialecticorum, in eandem rem, potissimum allegans id, quod negari non potest, videlicet ideo non posse Dialecticem prodesse Theologie, sed magis obesse, Quod eisdem vocabulis grammaticis longe aliter utatur Theologia quam Dialectica. Quomodo ergo, inquam, prodest Dialectica, cum, postquam accessero ad Theologiam, id vocabuli, quod in Dialectica sic significabat, cogar reiicere & aliam eius significationem accipere?» WA, Br.1, 150,21—28.

deduce from any other significations or put to the form of a syllogistic argument. On the contrary, *forma syllogistica* very often leads, according to Luther, to heresies for those who have rushed blindly into theology with it and who have wanted to reconcile everything by means of reason (per rationem) and to draw syllogistic conclusions *contra scipturam*. By means of this form and reason (hac forma et ratione) only troubles and faulty consequences are produced (26,₁₁₋₁₅, A). Hence in Luther's mind there is only one possibility left; one must adhere to the Word and speak according to it (in verbo manere et loqui) (17,₃₋₄, A).

The concept of belief proposed by Luther is not by nature an epistemic notion. If syllogistic logic were also valid in matters of faith, it would follow that a person who believes some religious proposition to be true, would as a rational being be obligated to believe everything which follows logically from the believed proposition by virtue of the universal validity of the syllogistic form. This is not the case, however, as examples of Trinitarian and Christological sophisms clearly display, where a false conclusion follows from true premises. Although a person believes that the propositions as premises are true, he is not according to Luther obligated to believe the logical consequences implied by them. Luther's notion of belief is here rather an example of a non-epistemic, i.e. a specific notion of *religious belief*.

When Luther says in the thesis 1: *Idem non est verum in diversis professionibus,* he does not seem to mean that theology would be »its own sphere» (sphaera). On the contrary, he emphasizes that to speak theologically is to speak »in new languages in the realm of faith *extra omnem sphaeram*» (T40). The examples in theses 29—36 are intended to show that peculiar modes of speaking of the diverse spheres of philosophy are not to be confused with each other. Nevertheless according to Luther, syllogistic logic would certainly be valid *within* each single sphere of philosophy (e.g. physics, geometry, etc.) The difference between theology and philosophy is, however, infinitely greater (in infinitum maior) than the differences between diverse spheres of philosophy (T39). This infinitely greater difference is to be seen in that »the syllogistic form or philosophical reason» does not hold in theology (T14). The »truth» of theological propositions is *extra, intra, supra, infra, citra, ultra omnem veritatem dialecticam* (T21). Therefore, one cannot simply say that theology and philosophy are »two different spheres,» which both have »their own peculiar knowledge and arguments», particularly since Luther does not know in his disputation any other meaning for the term 'argument' than the syllogistic argument.[49]

[49] Cf. *Hägglund,* 1955, 90.

APPENDIX

1. Etsi tenendum est, quod dicitur: Omne verum vero consonat, tamen idem non est verum in diversis professionibus.

2. In theologia verum est, verbum esse carnem factum, in philosophia simpliciter impossibile et absurdum.

3. Nec minus, imo magis disparata est praedicatio: Deus est homo, quam si dicas: Homo est asinus.

4. Sorbona, mater errorum, pessime definivit, idem esse verum in philosophia et theologia.

5. Impieque damnavit eos, qui contrarium disputaverunt.

6. Nam hac sententia abominabili docuit captivare articulos fidei sub iudicium rationis humanae.

7. Hoc erat aliud nihil, quam coelum et terram includere in suo centro aut grano milii.

8. Cum contra Paulus doceat, captivandum esse omnem intellectum (haud dubie et philosophiam) in obsequium Christi.

9. Facessant, dixit recte S. Ambrosius, dialectici, ubi credendum est piscatoribus apostolis.

10. Ex praedicabilium doctrina sequeretur pulchre: Deus est homo, ergo est animal rationale, sensitivum, animatum, corpus, substantia scilicet creata.

11. Sed quia christianis sobrie, et (ut Augustinus docet) secundum praescriptum est loquendum, tales consequentiae sunt simpliciter negandae.

12. Nec utendum nec fruendum est subtilibus istis inventis, de suppositione mediata et immediata, in rebus fidei.

13. Sunt enim logomachiae et kenophoniae in Ecclesia periculosae et scandalis plenae.

14. Sed ubiubi impingit vel forma syllogistica vel ratio philosophica, dicendum est ei illud Pauli: Mulier in Ecclesia taceat, et illud: Hunc audite.

15. Impingit quidem theologia in philosophiae regulas, sed ipsa vicissim magis in theologiae regulas.

16. Iste syllogismus expositorius: Pater in divinis generat. Pater est essentia divina. Ergo essentia divina generat, est bonus.

17. Et tamen praemissae sunt verae, conclusio falsa, et ita ex vero sequitur falsum contra philosophiam.

18. Iste syllogismus communis: Omnis essentia divina est pater. Filius est essentia divina. Ergo filius est pater, est bonus.

19. Sed praemissae sunt verae, et conclusio falsa, et verum vero hic prorsus non consonat.

20. Non quidem vitio formae syllogisticae, sed virtute et maiestate materiae, quae in angustias rationis seu syllogismorum includi non potest.

21. Ut quae sit non quidem contra, sed extra, intra, supra, infra, citra, ultra omnem veritatem dialecticam.

22. Iste syllogismus: Quidquid factum est caro, factum est creatura. Filius Dei est factus caro. Ergo filius Dei est factus creatura, est bonus in philosophia.

23. Ac si possit subtilibus kenophoniis sophistarum defendi, tamen non debet tolerari in ecclesia Dei.

24. Multo minus ista ferenda est: Omnis caro est creatura. Verbum est caro. Ergo verbum est creatura.

25. Nec ista: Omnis caro est creatura. Verbum non est creatura. Ergo verbum non est caro.

26. In his et similibus syllogismus est forma optima, sed nihil ad materiam.

27. Eundum ergo est ad aliam dialecticam et philosophiam in articulis fidei, quae vocatur verbum Dei et fides.

28. Hic sistendum est, et disputationes philosophiae contrarium concludentes pro ranarum coaxatione habendae.

29. Cogimur tamen etiam in aliis artibus negare, quod idem sit verum in omnibus.

30. Falsum est enim et error in genere ponderum, puncto et linea mathematica appendi posse pondera.

31. Falsum est et error in genere mensurarum, sextarium pedali vel ulnari mensura metiri.

32. Falsum est et error in genere linearum uncialis vel libralis comparartio.

33. Quin falsum et error est, quod linea recta et curva sint proportionales.

34. Et quadratores circuli, licet non falsum dicant, dum lineam rectam et curvam vocant utramque lineam.

35. Tamen hoc falsum est, si lineae rectae et curvae proportionem facere volunt.

36. Denique aliquid est verum in una parte philosophiae, quod tamen falsum est in alia parte philosophiae.

37. Humor humectat, est veritas in sphaera aëris, sed manifesta haeresis in sphaera ignis.

38. Ita per singula artificia vel potius opera, si transeas, nunquam invenias, idem esse verum in omnibus.

39. Quanto minus potest idem esse verum in philosophia et theologia, quarum distinctio in infinitum maior est, quam artium et operum.

40. Rectius ergo fecerimus, si dialectica seu philosophia in sua sphaera relictis discamus loqui novis linguis in regno fidei extra omnem sphaeram.

41. Aliqui futurum est, ut vinum novum in utres veteres mittamus, et utrumque perdamus, ut Sorbona fecit.

42. Affectus fidei exercendus est in articulis fidei, non intellectus philosophiae. Tum vere scietur, quid sit: Verbum caro factum est.

SOURCES

Luther, Martin

Disputatio de sententia: Verbum caro factum est (Joh. 1, 14) 11. Januar 1539. Weimarer Ausgabe, 39, II, 1—33. D. Martin Luthers Werke. Kritische Gesamtausgabe, Weimar 1883—.

Disputatio contra scholasticam theologiam, 1517, WA 1, 224—228.

Sermo Lutheri. In Natali Christi, A.1515, WA 1, 20—29.

Sermo in Festo Adscensionis Mariae, 1515, WA 1, 77—79.

De captivitate Babylonica ecclesiae praeludium 1520, WA 6, 497—573.

Luther's Randbemerkungen zu den Sentenzen des Petrus Lombardus, 1510/11, WA 9, 28—94.

Luther an Spalatin. Wittenberg, 22. Februar 1518. WA, Briefwechsel 1, 149—151.

Biel, Gabrielis

Collectorium circa quattuor libros Sententiarum. Ed. W. Werbeck and U. Hofmann. Prologus et Liber primus. J. C. B. Mohr (Paul Siebeck). Tübingen 1973.

The Centiloquim

The Centiloquium attributed to Ockham. Ed. Ph. Boehner. Fransiscan Studies, 1941, 58—70; 1942, 49—60; 146—157; 251—301.

Gregorius Ariminensis

Lectura super Primum et Secundum Sententiarum. Ed. A. D. Trapp, OSA, and V. Marcolino. Prologus et Dist. 1—6. Spätmittelalter und Reformation, Texte und Untersuchungen. Hrsg. H. Oberman, Band 6, Walter Gruyter, Berlin, New York 1981.

Ockham, Guillelmi de

Quaestiones in librum tertium sententiarum (reportatio). Opera Philosophica et Theologica. Opera Theologica VI. Ed. F. E. Kelley, G. I. Etzkorn. Editiones Instituti Fransiscani Universitatis S. Bonaventurae, New York 1982.

Ockham, William

Summa Logicae, Pars Prima. Ed. Ph. Boehner. The Fransiscan Institute St. Bonaventura, New York; E. Nauwelaerts, Louvain 1951.

Summa Logicae, Pars Secunda et Tertia Prima. Ed. Ph. Boehner, The

Fransiscan Institute St. Bonaventura, New York; E. Nauwelaerts, Louvain; F. Schöningh, Paderborn 1954.

Petrus Hispanus Portugalensis
Tractatus, called afterwards Summule Logicales. First Critical Edition from the Manuscripts with an Introduction. Ed. L. M. de Rijk. van Gorcum & Comp. N. V., Assen 1972.

Petrus Lombardus
Sententiae in quattuor libris distinctae Magistri Petri Lombardi, Parisiensis Episcopi. Liber I et II. P. P. Collegii S. Bonaventurae Ad Claras Aquas, Editio Tertia, Roma 1981.

Simon of Faversham
Quaestiones super libro elenchorum. Eds. S. Ebbesen, T. Izbicki, J. Longeway, F. del Punta, E. Serene, E. Stump. Pontificial Institute of Medieval Studies. Studies and Texts 60, Toronto 1984.

S. Thomae Aquinatis
Opera omnia, 4. Commentaria in Aristotelem et alios. F. Frommann Verlag, Stuttgart, Bad Constatt 1980.

Trutvetter, Jodocus
Summule totius logice, Erphord 1501.

LITERATURE

Adams, Marilyn McCord
1972   »Did Ockham Know of Material and Strict Implication? A Reconsideration,» Fransiscan Studies, 33, 5—37.

1982   »Relations, Inherence, and Subsistence: Was Ockham a Nestorian in Christology?,» Nous, 16, 62—75.

Asworth, E. J.
1974   Language and Logic in the Post-Medieval Period, Synthese historical library, 12, Dordrecht.

Boh, Ivan
1982   »Consequences,» CLMP, 300—314.

Boehner, Philotheus
1958   Collected Articles on Ockham. Ed. E. M. Buytaert. The Fransiscan Institute St. Bonaventure, New York; E. Nauwelaerts, Louvain; F. Schöningh, Paderborn. »Does Ockham Know of Material Implication,» 319—351; »The Medieval Crisis of Logic and the Author of the Centiloquium Attributed to Ockham,» 351—372; »Scholastic Theories of Truth,» 174—200.

The Cambridge History of Later Medieval Philosophy (CLMP)
1982   Ed. N. Kretzman, A. Kenny, J. Pinborg. Cambridge University Press, Cambridge, London, New York, New Rochelle, Melbourne, Sidney.

Copleston, F. C.
1972   A History of Medieval Philosophy. Methuen & Co Ltd, London.

Enders, Heinz
1975   Sprachlogische Traktate des Mittelalters und der Semantikbegriff. F. Schöningh, München, Paderborn, Wien (Veröffentlichungen des Grabmann-Institutes, Neue Folge, 20.)

Freddoso, Alfred J.
1983   »Logic, Ontology, and Ockham's Christology,» The New Scholasticism 57, 293—330.

Geach, Peter
1972   Logic Matters. Basil Blackwell, Oxford. »Nominalism,» 289—301.

Gilson, Etienne
1985   History of Christian Philosophy in the Middle Ages. Sheed and Ward, London 1955[1].

Grant, Edward
1982   »The Effect of the Condemnation of 1277,» CLMP, 537—539.

Green-Pedersen, Niels J.
1984   The Tradition of Topics in the Middle Ages. The commentaries on Aristotle's and Boethius' 'Topics'. Philosophia Verlag, München, Wien.

Hägglund, Bengt
1955   Theologie und Philosophie bei Luther und in der occamistischen Tradition. Luther Stellung zur Theorie von doppelten Wahrheit. C. W. K. Gleerup, Lund.

Kirjavainen, Heikki
1983   Uskon ja tiedon samanaikaisuus. Suomalaisen Teologisen Kirjallisuusseuran julkaisuja 137, Helsinki.

Kleineidam, Erich
1969   Universitas Studii Erffordensis. Überblicke über die Geschichte der Universität Erfurt im Mittelater 1392—1521. Teil II, 1460—1521. Erfurter theologische Studien 22. St. Benno Verlag, Leipzig.

Kneale, W. and Kneale, M.
1966   The Development of Logic. The Clarendon Press, Oxford.

Lerner, R. and Mahdi, M. (Eds.)
1963   Medieval Political Philosophy. Cornell University Press, Ithaca, New York. »Condemnation of 219 propositions,» trans. E. L. Fortin and P. D. O'Neill, 335—354.

Lienhard, Marc
1979   Martin Luthers christologisches Zeugnis. Entwicklung und Grundzüge seiner Christologie. Vandenhoeck & Ruprecht, Göttingen.

Lohr, Charles H.
1982   »The Medieval Interpretation of Aristotle,» CLMP, 80—98.

Lohse, Bernhard
1958   Ratio und Fides. Eine Untersuchung über die ratio in der Theologie Luthers. Vandenhoeck & Ruprecht, Göttingen.

Maierù, Alfonso
1984   »Logique et théologie trinitaire: Pierre d'Ailly,» Preuve et raisons a l'universitè de Paris; Logique, Ontologie et Théologie au XIV Siècle. Ed. Z. Kaluza, P. Vignaux, Paris.

1986   »Logique et théologie trinitaire dans le moyen-âge tardif: deux solutions en présence,» The Editing of Theological and Philosophical Texts from the Middle Ages. Acts of the Conference Arranged by the Department of Classical Languages, University of Stockholm, 29—31

178

August 1984. Ed. Monica Asztalos. Acta Universitas Stockholmiensis. Almqvist & Wiksell International, Stockholm, 185—201.

Maurer, Armand A.
1982   Medieval Philosophy. Pontificial Institute of Medieval Studies, Toronto 1962[1].

Moster, Walter
1983   »Luthers Verhältnis zur theologischen und philosophischen Über-lieferung,» Leben und Werke Martin Luthers von 1526 bis 1546. Fest-gabe zu seinem 500. Geburtstag. Hrsg. Helmar Junghans. Band I, II. Vandenhoeck & Ruprecht, Göttingen.

Oberman, Heiko
1963   The Harvest of Medieval Theology. Gabriel Biel and Late Medieval Nominalism. Harvard University Press, Cambridge, Massachusetts.

Rijk, L. M. de
1962   Logica Modernorum. A Contribution to the History of Early Terminist Logic. Wijsgerige Teksten en Studies, VI. Van Gorcum & Comp. N. V., Assen. Vol. I, On the Twelfth Century Theories of Fallacy.

1967   Logica Modernorum. Vol. II, Part I, The Origin and Early Development of the Theory of Supposition.

1972   »Pope John XXI (Peter of Spain) as the Author of the socalled Summule Logicales,» *Petrus Hispanus,* 1972, IX—XXIV; »The Life and Works of Peter of Spain,» *Petrus Hispanus,* 1972, XXIV—XLIII.

1982   »The Origin of the Theory of the Properties of Terms,» CLMP, 161—173.

Schwarz, Reinhard
1966   »Gott ist Mensch. Zur Lehre von der Person Christi bei den Ockha-misten und bei Luther,» Zeitschrift für Theologie und Kirche 63, 288—351.

Serene, Eileen
1982   »Demonstrative Science,» CLMP, 496—517.

Spade, Paul V.
1982   »The Semantics of Terms,» CLMP, 188—196.

Stump, Eleonore
1982   »Topics: their development and absorption into consequences,» CLMP, 273—299.